Lawn Sprinklers
A Do-It-Yourself Guide

Lawn Sprinklers
A Do-It-Yourself Guide

Richard L. Austin

TAB BOOKS
Blue Ridge Summit, PA

FIRST EDITION
FIRST PRINTING

Copyright © 1990 by TAB BOOKS
Printed in the United States of America

Library of Congress Cataloging-in-Publication Data

Austin, Richard L.
Lawn sprinklers : a do-it-yourself guide / by Richard L. Austin.
p. cm.
ISBN 0-8306-2093-1   ISBN 0-8306-3193-3 (pbk.)
1. Lawns—Irrigation—Equipment and supplies—Handbooks, manuals,
etc. 2. Sprinklers—Handbooks, manuals, etc. 3. Sprinkler
irrigation—Equipment and supplies—Handbooks, manuals, etc.
I. Title.
SB433.2.A86 1990
635.9′64787—dc20   89-29129
                                                         CIP

TAB BOOKS offers software for
sale. For information and a catalog,
please contact TAB Software Department,
Blue Ridge Summit, PA 17294-0850.

Questions regarding the content of this book
should be addressed to:

Reader Inquiry Branch
TAB BOOKS
Blue Ridge Summit, PA 17294-0214

Acquisitions Editor: Kimberly Tabor
Book Editor: Nina E. Barr
Production: Katherine Brown

Cover photograph courtesy of
Rain Bird Sprinkler Manufacturing Corporation
145 N. Grand Avenue
Glendora, CA 91740

Contents

Acknowledgments

THE AUTHOR WISHES TO EXPRESS APPRECIATION TO BUCKNER IRRIGAtion Systems for the use of technical information from its irrigation design manual; to the TORO Company, Irrigation Division, and Rain Bird Sales, Incorporated, Turf Division, for the review of their planning and installation guides; and, especially to Hardie Irrigation for the extensive use of information on the RainJet homeowner system and the state-of-the-art Drip Irrigation System. The addresses and telephone numbers of these companies are listed in Appendix C.

Introduction

WELCOME TO THE WORLD OF HOME LAWN WATERING SYSTEMS! IF YOU HAVE made the decision to install your own landscape irrigation, you have made a good choice. Full or partial automatic lawn irrigation is no longer an item of luxury—it is one of necessity!

The massive drought of 1988 was experienced by many parts of the nation. Recovery from its damaging effects will be slow and time consuming. From this experience, the need to conserve and regulate the use of water has moved public conservation programs to the forefront. Many cities now impose severe penalties for the overuse of water for lawns and landscapes.

The solution for the homeowner is simple. Install a watering system that conserves water and meets municipal requirements, both now and in the future. Stop wasting water and energy with ineffective hoses and hand sprinklers.

A home lawn watering system will improve the value of your property and conserve valuable moisture at the same time. With your system in place, you can direct the delivery of water to precise locations on your property. You no longer have to use cumbersome hand sprinklers that do not always deliver water where you want.

This how-to handbook presents the information you need to complete your project in easy-to-follow steps. The first chapter covers the predesign considerations that help you determine the best system for your needs. It overviews the different systems available and illustrates the way you should select the program that is best for you. The issues of sprinkler coverage patterns, watering rates, and basic hydraulics are reviewed to help you through the first, simple stages to success.

From predesign considerations, you will move into basic design and layout in the second chapter. After a basic evaluation and measurement of your site, you will design the actual locations of sprinkler heads, circuit valves, and system controllers. Even the issues of pipe system layout are illustrated in these easy-to-follow steps.

After you have made a thorough evaluation of your property and have designed a custom system, you will learn how to install your system. The third chapter covers the types of systems you might desire and shows how each can become a part of your garden program.

If you are part of the rapidly growing audience of do-it-yourselfers, this handbook will be a perfect guide into the world of lawn watering systems. With it you will be able to create the perfect weekend project, and in doing so, respond to the need for water conservation and the more precise watering needs for home landscapes.

Saves Time

You will not need to spend long hours watering with garden hoses. You won't have to worry about when to move a hose or how long the water has been running. An automatic system will do the remembering for you.

Saves Water

A properly designed and installed sprinkler system will water precisely where water is needed, when it is needed.

Saves Plants

Precisely measured and properly timed watering promotes optimum plant growth. This generates a lush green landscape and increases the attractiveness of your property.

Increases Property Values

In addition to creating a more attractive property, a lawn sprinkler system will increase the return on your investment. A properly designed and installed system will quickly add value to your home and landscape.

Following are some of the most commonly asked questions about home sprinkler systems.

- *Will an automatic sprinkler system do as good a job of watering as I can do by hand?*
  It will do a better job of watering your lawn and landscape because the system will place the right amount of water on lawn and garden areas.

- *Will a system use more water than I use by hand watering?*
  No. It will use less water. Most systems deliver water so precisely to your landscape, that you will actually need less water than before.

- *I live in an area of high rainfall—greater than 50 inches each year. Do I really need a lawn sprinkler system?*
  Unfortunately, nature does not work in perfect cycles. Most lawns and landscapes need exact, timed watering cycles to maintain lush growth. In a dry season, when there is little or no rain, your landscape can suffer severe damage after a few days without water. You need a sprinkler system to maintain accurate and precise watering cycles.

- *Are there different types of systems available?*
  There are basically two types of lawn sprinkler systems: automatic and manual. Both have specific applications to today's lawn and garden needs. The most popular approach is to apply both technologies to fit your needs.

- *Will a lawn sprinkler system really save me time?*
  An automatic lawn sprinkler system will save you a great deal of time. It can be programmed to operate when you are busy or away from home. A manual system also will save you time, but not as much as an automatic system.

- *How do I know what type of system is best for me?*
  Your system should be customized to fit your specific watering needs, because every landscapes situation is different. If you have a large landscaped area with many different types of plants, a fully automatic system is probably best. If you have a medium-sized landscape, a combination automatic and manual system might fit your needs better. If you have a small landscape, a manual (drip) system might fulfill your requirements.

- *Can I really save money by installing the system myself?*
  Yes. The manufacturing technology of today has made the design and installation of the system very easy for almost everyone. With professional help from your local plumbing contractor (to connect to the city water supply), you can install most systems without the need for heavy equipment.

- *Is a lawn sprinkler system too complicated to operate?*
  No. Almost all of the materials you will need are available readily from your local hardware store or building supply dealer. With easy-to-follow instructions and convenient control units, every system can be designed and installed for ease of operation.

1

Where To Begin

WHEN YOU BEGIN TO DESIGN YOUR HOME LAWN SRINKLER SYSTEM, IT IS VERY important for you to focus on four important factors:

1. The type of system you want
2. The sprinkler coverage patterns
3. The watering rates you desire
4. The basic hydraulics

TYPES OF SYSTEMS

Three types of lawn irrigation systems are available for your consideration.

The first type is the fully automatic, high-pressure system. It is comprised of high-energy impact rotors, pop-up heads, and flower-bed bubblers that deliver moisture on cue without supervision. Through an elaborate network of pipes, it keeps your lawn bright and green during the growing season. It requires little effort on your part because it has sophisticated electronic controls. The main characteristic of this system is that it does the watering work for you.

The second type is the manual, high-pressure system. It is comprised of a permanent piping network with hand-located heads and special watering heads that you can change and relocate as you desire. Electric control boxes are not required, nor is an elaborate piping system. You regulate the watering, and you control the system features. It is not fully automatic, nor is it fully manual. It is the "in between" system of compromise.

The third type is a manual system which is gaining in popularity and is called the *drip irrigation system*. It is very convenient for smaller landscapes, vegetable gardens, and patio plantings. Specifically tailored for small home gardens and the precise watering of ground-cover plants and flowers, it comes in easy-to-assemble kits or interchangeable components. No major construction is needed with this type of system. Installation is as easy as placing a small hose system throughout a planting bed or small lawn area and connecting it to a water hydrant. You then would adjust the faucet to the desired flow and pressure, and the plants receive the exact amount of water they need. This simple, uncomplicated application of moisture to plants is resource conservative because of the small amount of water it uses. Many experts consider it the lawn sprinkler system of the future.

If you are trying to decide which system is best for you, review the chart in Table 1-1 to compare the seven important basic requirements. The high-pressure or the manual systems are excellent additions to your landscape. Selection should depend mostly on what you, the homeowner, need or desire in a lawn watering system.

A convenient compromise might be the best approach if the final decision becomes a difficult one. Parts of your property might benefit from automated components, while other areas can receive the personal attention a manual unit allows.

Regardless of the system you select, the design approach will be related directly to the sprinkler coverage patterns, watering rates, and basic hydraulics. Each of these issues will control the quality of the system and the overall value it adds to your landscape.

Table 1-1. The System Comparison Checklist.

Characteristics	Automatic System	Manual System
Trenching	R	R/O
Sophisticated Heads	R	NR
Manual Location of Heads	NR	R
Piping Network	R	R
Electric Controls	R	NR
Ease of Replacement/Repair	D	ND
Add-on/Expansion	D	ND

R = required; NR = not required; R/O = required or optional
D = difficult; ND = not difficult.

THE SPRINKLER COVERAGE PATTERNS

The proper location of sprinkler heads is the secret to any successful system. You must distribute water to your landscape in a uniform manner to avoid severe problems with attractiveness and plant growth. Uneven watering will create uneven growth cycles for foundation plantings and lawn grasses. Without the proper placement of heads, lawns could have areas of lush green and areas of dormant brown occurring side by side. Shrub rows and flower beds could have uneven heights and might become unsightly features in your garden.

Coverage patterns are rectilinear or circular and are controlled by the following:

- The radius of throw.
- The water pattern. (Fig. 1-1)
- The water trajectory. (Figs. 1-2 through 1-5)

A number of important factors determine the uniformity of water coverage, most of which you can control by the selection of reliable equipment. These factors include the following items:

- The type of sprinkler head and nozzle.

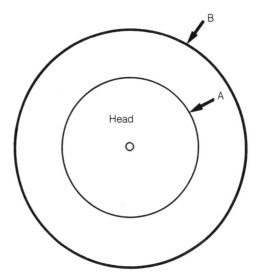

Fig. 1-1. The selection of sprinkler heads for your system is very important based upon their ability to deliver moisture to your landscape. Many heads deliver the majority of the water to an area nearest the center of the spray pattern (Area A). The edge (Area B) receives less moisture.

- The type of spray heads.
- The type of stream heads.
- The spacing of the sprinklers.
- The operating pressure of the sprinklers.
- The slope of your yard.
- The spacing pattern of the heads.

The Type of Sprinkler Head and Nozzle

The type of sprinkler head primarily is controlled by the type of nozzle it has, which might be a single nozzle or a double nozzle. The discharge trajectory of the head is related to its nozzle, and is called a *spray* or *stream nozzle*.

Spray Heads

Spray sprinkler heads are available in stationary or pop-up varieties. Stationary varieties do not have any working parts which would break or need repair. The pop-up types have only two working parts—the body and the nozzle. Stationary sprays have a solid body and usually you attach them directly to a piping system via a small riser. Pop-up units come in various heights depending on how they are to function in your design. (See Figs. 1-6 through 1-12.)

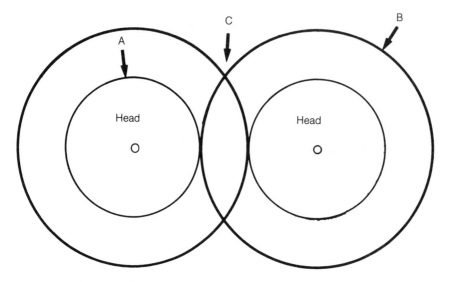

Fig. 1-2. To solve the moisture deficiency in the outer portion of the spray areas, overlapping of patterns is required. Area B then will receive the necessary moisture because of the overlap in area C.

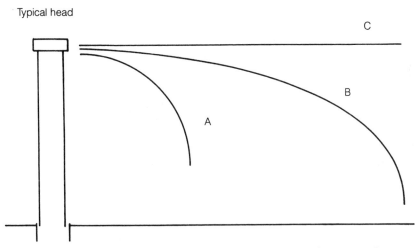

Typical head

Fig. 1-3. The operating pressure of the sprinkler system is very important. A system of too little pressure will "under deliver" water to your landscape (A). A system under too much pressure will "over deliver" water to your landscape (C). Water under extreme pressure often evaporates before it reaches the landscape. A system under proper pressure will maintain an accurate radius of throw (B).

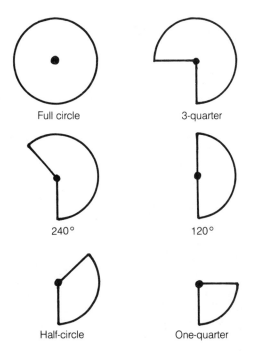

Full circle

3-quarter

240°

120°

Half-circle

One-quarter

Fig. 1-4. The various patterns of degrees that can be created for the radius of throw are typically 90, 120, 180, 240, 270, and 360 (full circle) degrees.

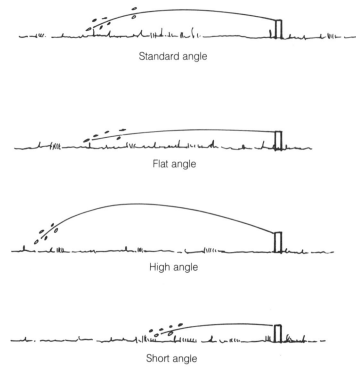

Standard angle

Flat angle

High angle

Short angle

Fig. 1-5. Develop various trajectory angles to deliver water more efficiently to your plants. Use a low, flat angle to reach under small trees and shrubs. Apply a modified angle to groundcover areas and flower beds. Use a high angle on stream heads to deliver water over an obstruction.

Fig. 1-6. The stationary head is located on the edge of the lawn area. With a full-circle spray pattern, it can water the grass and the groundcovers in the adjacent planting bed.

Fig. 1-7. This is a typical stationary spray head located on an 18-inch riser. The spray is soft and does not damage the delicate roses growing in this bed. The angle of adjustment in this application is 180 degrees. Because it is next to a structure, it should not be a safety hazard.

Fig. 1-8. This stationary spray head has been overgrown with lawn grass. If you live in an area where creeping grass varieties are popular, the use of this type of head for lawns is not recommended. The grass eventually will block the ability of the head to deliver its spray.

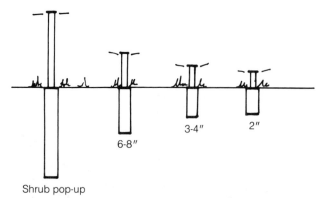

Shrub pop-up

Fig. 1-9. The most practical spray heads for today's landscape are the pop-up varieties. They rise from the body unit to deliver the water, then retract out of the way when completed. Several pop-up heights are available, depending upon the need.

The height chart in Table 1-2 will assist you in selecting the pop-up units you need for your program.

Nozzles for the spray heads screw directly onto the unit head, with some models attaching directly to a riser. You easily can change, replace, or clean them, and you can adjust them to control the spray patterns you need. Low-gallonage nozzles are available now to restrict the amount of water you use to almost half the amount you use with regular nozzles. These nozzles are the first choice for most systems when there is a clay soil or if local water-use codes demand restricted water use.

The only disadvantage to spray heads are their limitations regarding the distance of throw. The more pressure you apply to these head types, the more water they waste. This result is because increased pressure creates smaller water droplets, not more radius of throw. Smaller droplets evaporate more rapidly and will waste the precious moisture.

Stream Heads

These units often are called *stream rotors* because they rotate from the impact created by the stream of water coming from the nozzle. Some

Table 1-2. Pop-up Selection Chart.

Pop-up Height	General Application
2″	Short height grass
3″	Medium height grass
4″	Tall lawn grass
5″	Ground covers, short
6″	Small shrubs

A

B

Fig. 1-10A and B. This typical lawn pop-up unit allows the head to spray above the height of your lawn grass. The housing material (A) is sturdy plastic and protects the working parts. When you turn on the water, the spray unit ''pops up'' (B) to deliver the moisture.

Fig. 1-11A and B. The spray from this pop-up will reach a wide pattern to supply your lawn with moisture. This head (A) has been positioned next to the curb to water a newly seeded area. It will have a 180 degree arc. This side view of a pop-up spray illustrates where the name ''spray unit'' is derived (Courtesy of James Hardie Irrigation).

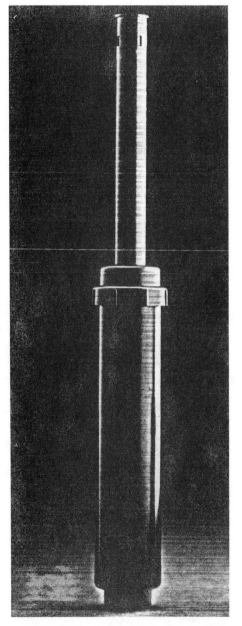

Fig. 1-12. This maximum height pop-up unit allows the head to reach above groundcover masses and small shrubs to deliver water over the top of the plants. Courtesy of Buckner Irrigation.

types of stream heads are gear driven but these are not recommended for residential use. They are expensive and require almost continuous maintenance.

Stream units pop up to about three inches above the lawn to deliver the water. The distance of throw can be large, and often a few stream heads can cover a very large section of your landscape. (See Figs. 1-13 through 1-18.)

The Spacing of the Sprinklers

The greater the spacing of the sprinklers, the greater the problem with uniformity, especially in areas of frequent high-wind velocities. The National Weather Service can provide you with the monthly averages for the winds in your area. Ask for the Local Climatology Data, Annual Summary, which will indicate the months that will have the highest winds.

The spacing of the heads controls the delivery of moisture to your plants by the pattern of the water leaving the head. The designs of some heads deliver water to the outside of the coverage pattern while others spray closer to the head.

Incorrectly spaced heads will cause weak or dead portions of lawn, groundcovers, or shrubs. If you fertilize regularly, the nutrients will not reach the plant root systems unless you achieve proper spacing. To control the coverage patterns and to insure that all areas are receiving mois-

Fig. 1-13. This is a very popular unit for delivering water to your landscape. It is available in a variety of designs to fit your needs. This is a hand-mounted, impact unit which attaches to a garden hose.

Fig. 1-14. The impact unit is now placed in a protective housing and "pops-up" to deliver water in a heavy stream.

Fig. 1-15. The basic rotor pop-up is the same as the hose end attachment, but now it has been designed as part of the automatic system.

Fig. 1-16. The rotor spray unit fits the same riser components as typical spray units.

Fig. 1-17. This rotor spray unit rises from the housing to spray the lawn, with energy supplied by the pressure from the water.

Fig. 1-18. After completing its spray cycle, the unit recedes into the protective housing unit. Mowing over it is not a problem if you have installed it properly.

ture, overlapping is necessary. Overlapping is not a waste of water; it is a technique in the design to direct the distribution of moisture evenly throughout your landscape. (Most industry professionals figure a sprinkler head provides effective moisture for two-thirds of the pattern. Thus, overlapping is necessary.)

The Operating Pressure of the Sprinklers

Water pressure for your area must be sufficient to allow the heads to function properly. You can test this factor easily with a pressure gauge borrowed from your local hardware store or plumber.

Operating pressure is related in terms of pounds per square inch (PSI) and is converted to gallons per minute (GPM). Both of these factors are important because they affect water as it leaves the sprinkler head. A change in either of these factors immediately will change the diameter of the coverage patterns for your system.

Pressure that is too low will create large water droplets and a smaller-than-needed coverage pattern. On the other hand, pressure that is too high forms smaller droplets that surface winds might carry off.

The size of the water droplets is very important. Large droplets

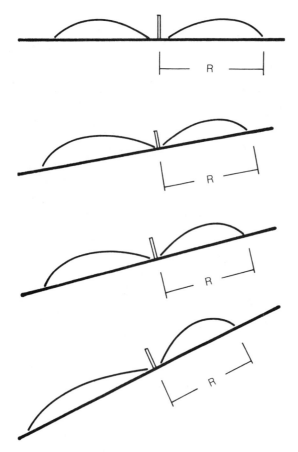

Fig. 1-19. The slope of your property is important to the spacing pattern. Place heads closer to the uphill side of the lawn to overlap the radius of throw (R). Photograph courtesy of Irrigation Systems Design Manual; Buckner Irrigation Systems.

might "doughnut" and miss parts of your lawn or garden. Tiny droplets might evaporate too soon after leaving the head.

An ideal operating pressure is available for every sprinkler head today. The manufacturer of the heads will state this information directly on the package.

The Slope of Your Yard

The water that leaves a sprinkler head has a force behind it. Combine this force with the affects of gravity and the downhill part of your lawn might receive too much or too little water. In some cases, even severe erosion can occur. Another important factor is the trajectory of the stream of

Fig. 1-20. Sprinkler heads aligned perpendicular to the slope do not damage the lawn grasses (A). Heads aligned to the uphill side (B) might cause erosion as the force of the water stream strikes the soil (C). Courtesy of Irrigation System's design manual; Buckner Irrigation Systems.

water. Serious damage always will result to your plants if you do not align the heads properly to the slope.

Heads should be perpendicular to the surface of the slope as a normal guide. They should never be more than 10 degrees away from normal. (See Figs. 1-19 and 1-20.)

The Spacing Pattern of the Heads

Magic formulas to determine sprinkler-head spacing patterns do not exist. The shape of your yard and the desired distribution of water are the two most important factors to consider. Individual manufacturers often have specific requirements for their products. These products, however, also might have limitations. Most sprinkler heads, when selected within the range of the manufacturer's recommendations, will perform adequately for your needs.

Although head models differ from manufacturer to manufacturer, they all are designed to deliver water to your lawn. Spacing patterns, therefore, should vary with your specific need. Make sure you match your needs against the manufacturer's suggested use and requirements for the head.

The two basic head design patterns are square and triangular. Preference for either pattern is mostly personal, but many designers choose the triangular because often it requires fewer heads to water a landscaped area. (See Figs. 1-21 and 1-22.)

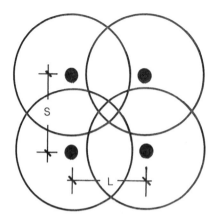

Fig. 1-21. The basic overlap percentage for the square layout is 50% of the diameter coverage. Recommended spacing (S or L) in percentage of diameter of sprinkler coverage is as follows:

No wind—55% of diameter
4 mph wind—50% of diameter
8 mph wind—45% of diameter
S = spacing between sprinklers
L = spacing between lateral lines

Artwork courtesy of Lawn Sprinkler System design guide, Rain Bird Sprinkler Mfg. Corp.

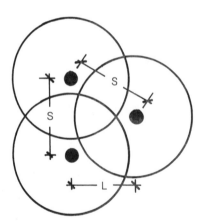

Fig. 1-22. The basic overlap percentage for the triangular layout is 55% of diameter of coverage. Recommended spacing(s) in percentage of diameter of sprinkler coverage is as follows:

no wind—60% of diameter
4 mph wind—55% of diameter
8 mph wind—50% of diameter
S = spacing between sprinklers
L = spacing between rows = $.86 \times S$

Information courtesy of Lawn Sprinkler System's design guide, Rain Bird Sprinkler Mfg. Corp.

WATERING RATES

The length of time it takes to deliver a specific amount of water to your lawn is called the *precipitation rate (PR)*. It is like rainfall, which is also measured in inches per hour. When a thunderstorm delivers a two-inch rain in two hours, it is reported that one inch of rain fell in one hour of time. You should think of your sprinkler precipitation in the same way. When your system delivers water to a depth of one inch in one hour, the PR is one inch/hour. (See Table 1-3.)

This rate, theoretically represents the amount of water delivered from a given group of sprinklers within a specific space. System designers use PR as a benchmark multiplier to calculate the efficiency of water delivery to a landscaped area. For almost twenty years, it also has guided the development of commercial sprinkler systems.

PR is the equivalent of the amount of water you need to handle your system on a daily basis. It is very important to maintain adequate soil moisture during the peak growing seasons of the plants in a landscape. When soil moisture fluctuates too often, your lawn grasses and shrub plantings might wilt.

Manufacturers calculate and convert watering rates into the inches of water your landscape area might need each week. They then compare these numbers to the inches per hour discharged from the sprinkler heads in your system. This final numbered product becomes the precipitation rate, and guides the number of hours per week your sprinkler system needs to run to maintain your lawn and plantings.

Modern systems are much more efficient in the distribution of water to a given area. Technological advances in equipment design have allowed the use of more accurate sprinkler heads. These new heads are capable of pinpoint accuracy. The need for a "broadcast" system to watering has been eliminated along with the dependence of detailed PR calculations.

With the aid of computers and systems modeling, most equipment manufacturers have been able to calculate the PR for you. When you purchase your equipment, the manufacturer's recommendation for spacing and distance of throw already have taken this factor into account. (I will

Table 1-3. Water Facts.

1 cubic ft. = 62.4 lbs.
1 cubic in. = 0.03605 lb.
1 gallon = 8.36 lbs.
1 cubic ft. = 7.48 gallons

discuss the specific calculations for water use in your system in chapter 2.)

BASIC HYDRAULICS

The study of the behavior of liquids at rest and in motion is known as *hydraulics*. It is one of the most important factors that you must consider in the design of any home sprinkler system. When the hydraulic flow is improper, the overall performance of the system will be poor.

Following are five important concerns regarding hydraulics:

- The available water supply and quantity.
- The static and working water pressures.
- The water-flow characteristics.
- The sprinkler performance characteristics.
- The size of the selected pipe.

The Available Water Supply and Quantity

As mentioned earlier under operating pressure, you easily can test the water supply you have available to your home. This test determines the main factors of PSI and GPM. When you begin your design task, you will complete an exercise to calculate GPM from the measured pressure per square inch for your property.

The Static and Working Water Pressures

Static water pressure, called *hydrostatics*, is an indication of the potential pressure available within a closed sprinkler system, or one where water remains at rest. Working water pressure (*hydrodynamics*), on the other hand, is the pressure at any given point as water flows past. This pressure, also called *dynamic water pressure (DWP)*, differs from static water pressure (SWP) in that it varies throughout the sprinkler system due to *friction losses* as the water moves along the pipe. (Fig. 1-23.)

Every sprinkler head needs a minimum amount of pressure to operate properly. The manufacturer supplies this information and it must be strictly followed. When you use too many sprinkler heads within a circuit, which is the most common design error, a severe pressure loss results. With working or dynamic water pressure, energy loss is caused by water flowing against the surface of the pipe, water moving past a fitting or valve (causing turbulence), and water moving out of the sprinkler head. Working pressure is always less than static pressure.

The important factor to remember is the pressure (energy) loss in the

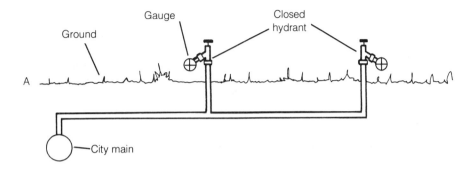

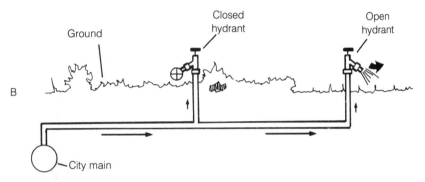

Fig. 1-23. (A) When pressure gauges are placed on hydrants and the water is turned off, the readings on the gauges will be the same. This is *static water pressure* (SWP). (B) When one gauge is removed and the water is turned on, the remaining will indicate the working pressure for a sprinkler system. Information courtesy of Irrigation System's design manual, Buckner Irrigation Systems.

system equals the static pressure minus the working pressure. The static pressure of the system will be a given factor measurable by a simple gauge. In some areas, city offices can supply you with the static pressure at the main service line. The working pressure, therefore, must be sufficient to operate the sprinkler heads selected for your system.

The Water-Flow Characteristics

The flow of a given volume of water in a lawn sprinkler system is measured in gallons per minute. The speed (velocity) of the flow is measured in linear feet per second and must be controlled to avoid damage to a piping system. The manufacturer determines the operating velocity of the flow requirements for any given system of sprinkler heads. It is related directly to GPM and PSI.

For plastic piping systems, a velocity of five to seven feet per second (maximum) in the lateral lines and five feet per second (maximum) in the

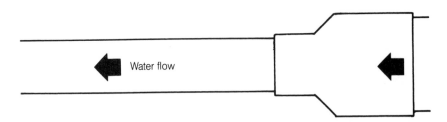

Fig. 1-24. The velocity of the water moving through the piping network is important to the performance of the sprinkler system. The relationship between the speed of the water and the recommended PSI is as follows:

Sprinkler GPM	Recommended PSI
2	20-25
4	30-35
6	35-40
8	35-40
10	40-45
15	40-45

Information courtesy of USDA, Soil Conservation Service.

main line is desirable. You can use the velocity flowchart in the appendix section to check the feet per second for various sizes of system pipes. (See Fig. 1-24.)

Velocity of flow is the speed at which water moves within the components of the sprinkler system. You can control it in a sprinkler system by using the following procedures:

1. Regulate the quantity of water flowing through the pipe.
2. Regulate the diameter of the pipe through which the water flows.
3. Regulate the pressure loss within the network of pipes.

(See the Chart of Pipe Sizes and GPM-Velocity, Table 1-4.)

Table 1-4. Pipe Sizes and GPM—Velocity.

Pipe Size (Inches)	GPM-Velocity
.5	1-6
3/4	7-10
1	11-16
1.5	27-35

GPM = Gallons Per Minute

Information courtesy of Rain Bird Sales, Inc.

The Sprinkler Performance Characteristics

This factor relates specifically to the mechanical requirements of the individual heads. If a specific amount of water pressure is required to deliver water to a given area of lawn, then specific hydraulics must be designed into the system. Each of the manufacturing companies listed in the appendix section supply the mechanical requirements of the heads they market for home sprinkler use.

The Size of the Selected Pipe

The pipe systems designed for a home lawn sprinkler system must be sized to supply the correct amount of water to each of the operating heads. If the most distant head at the end of a specific sprinkler circuit has sufficient pressure to operate properly, then the intermediate heads probably will be sufficient also. The correct pipe sizes for your system will be developed in the design tasks that follow.

SELECTING THE COMPONENTS

Once you have decided upon the sprinkler system you want, selecting the right equipment is the next important step. For the do-it-yourselfer, the components are readily available in most hardware or building supply stores. Basically, lawn sprinkler components are classified into the following categories.

- Sprinkler heads.
- Valves.
- Controllers.
- Pipe materials and fittings.

Sprinkler Heads

A *sprinkler head* is the device that distributes the water over your lawn or landscape. A variety of models and types are available from which to choose to customize your sprinkler applications. The choice of head will depend upon how you want the water to reach your plants. Following are the types of heads available for your property:

- Bed spray head.
- Shrub bubbler/flood head.
- Lawn spray head.
- Stream rotary head.

Bed Spray Head. These heads throw water to a relatively small area in a flat, low angle. Patterns range from full circle to quarter circle, and usually should not exceed a throw radius of four to five feet.

You should limit the bed spray head to shrub or groundcover areas and narrow planter boxes. Install it just above the ground but beneath the crown of the shrubs. If it is too high or too low, water will not disperse to the plants adequately. If the shrub area eventually will be a dense growth area, a different type of head might be required to water the plants.

Maintenance of the basic bed spray head is limited to a periodic cleaning of the nozzle. If it becomes clogged with dirt or debris, you can easily remove and clean it. If it becomes damaged, you can remove or replace the nozzle or riser easily.

Most bed spray heads have been copper or brass with similar materials for the rise units. The newer models, however, are made of lightweight and less expensive plastics. These newer plastic materials are just as efficient as the metal units and are much easier to install.

Shrub Bubbler/Flood Head. This type of shrub head is designed to deliver a large quantity of water to a delicate area of the garden by flooding. The term "bubbler" has been derived from the sound it makes when water comes out of the head. Essentially, the bubbler head and the flood head are the same.

You should limit the use of this type of head to small areas of the garden or landscape. You should never expect the bubbler head to cover much area. As water flows from the head, the ground next to the head will soak up the moisture. When the ground around the head is saturated, severe overflow and erosion might occur. This type of unit might have a tendency to waste water if you do not control it properly.

Install it far enough above the ground to be effective. If it is too low, it might collect debris from the planting bed and become clogged. When clogged, you can clean and replace it easily. (See Fig. 1-25)

Lawn Spray Head. Two types of lawn spray heads are available: *pop-up* and *stationary*. Either head will water your lawn accurately and effectively. Selection will depend upon the type of unit you want for your property. (See Figs. 1-6 to 1-13 and Table 1-2.)

In a pop-up unit the force of the water pushes the head up out of the body housing to start the watering cycle. When the pressure is decreased, it returns to the housing unit. It is constructed with a flat flange to prevent grass growth from reaching the nozzle. In areas where creeping grasses are popular, the flange might not be effective.

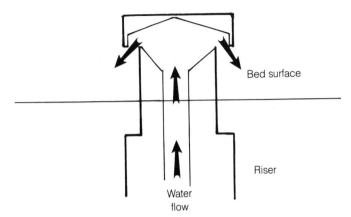

Bed surface

Riser

Water flow

Fig. 1-25. This head type has neither a spray or a stream nozzle. It merely "bubbles" out to flood a specific bed area. You should not use it in lawn areas.

This head is used to water lawn areas where uniform coverage and maximum control over the radius of throw is desirable. The available nozzle varieties range from fine sprays to the raindrop effects. Materials range from brass to plastic.

Depending upon your lawn grass, the maintenance requirements are limited to nozzle cleaning. If your grass grows quickly, you might need to trim the grass around the head more frequently.

The stationary lawn head is a fixed unit and has no moving parts. This type of head was the first type ever used in lawn sprinkler designs and is still used today. High-tech manufacturing and nozzle variety virtually have replaced this head type.

Stream Rotary Head. Like the shrub spray head, the rotary heads come in pop-up and stationary units. It is one of the more effective watering devices and has specific application to large areas of lawn and garden development.

The pop-up rotary has a characteristic lid or cap covering the housing unit. When the water pressure is high, the unit pops-up and distributes water to a large area of up to fifty feet in radius. When the pressure is low, the head retreats to its housing chamber.

Unlike the pop-up spray head, the pop-up rotary is a more mechanically complicated unit. In addition to the impact arm which moves the unit in its pattern of spray, there are two nozzles, retracting springs, and, in some units, bearing assemblies. Although manufacturing technology is making these units more efficient, they will require more maintenance and care than other types of heads.

These heads distribute water to a landscape by the high pressure within the system. As water, under pressure, passes through the nozzle, it strikes an impact arm which pushes the head to the preset angle. The constantly repeating impacts produce the steady rotation of the unit to the desired pattern of throw.

Stationary or above, rotaries are used primarily in quick-coupling designs. The head design is essentially the same as the pop-up rotary, without the housing unit. The distance of throw and the ability to reach large areas is the primary function of this type of head.

Most of the units manufactured today require relatively little maintenance. The more complex the unit, however, the more maintenance will be a part of your program. Some units have a tendency to collect dirt

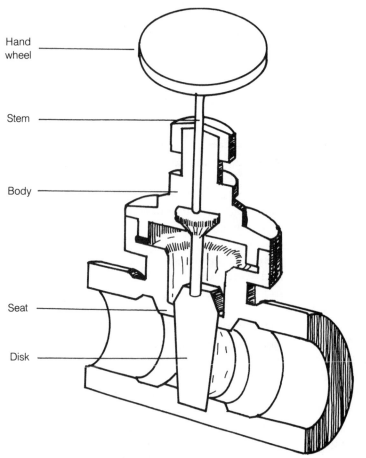

Hand wheel

Stem

Body

Seat

Disk

Fig. 1-26. This cut away illustration shows the different parts of a manual valve unit. It, too, plays an important role in the overall system design.

within the body housing, which prevents the pop-up from retracting completely. Grass should be kept away from the cap and body housing to reduce this problem. Fortunately, the modern plastic pop-up rotaries are disassembled easily for replacing broken parts and cleaning.

Valves

The term *valve* applies to a mechanical device that controls the flow of water, on or off. The most common valve found around the home is the simple faucet, which is found in bathrooms and kitchens. The outside hydrant is also a common water-flow valve.

The most often used valve in a lawn sprinkler system is the *gate valve*. It is attached next to the city water supply outlets. It might have a wheel handle for hand turning or a cross handle which operates with a key. Some of these units are made with drain plugs built into the housing. These plugs are used on the "down stream" side of the flow to help remove the water from the system during the winter. (See Fig. 1-26.)

The second major valve within a sprinkler system is the main control valve that regulates the individual piping circuits. You can operate this unit manually or by electricity activated from the controller unit. Often,

Fig. 1-27. Although small in size, this heavy brass back-flow unit does a big job for your system. It prevents contaminated water (debris and lawn chemicals) from flowing back into the water supply system.

this valve type is grouped with other units and housed in a valve box. The same principle that operates the main control valve is used to operated a "remote-control valve" at a distant location from the main units.

A third important valve is the *anti-siphon* or *back-flow preventer*, which often is called a "swing valve" by city water personnel. Its primary function is to prevent water in the sprinkler system from draining back into the city water supply. Although the mechanics of this unit are simple, its function within the system is very important. (See Fig. 1-27.)

Another type of valve used in some manual system designs is the quick-coupling valve. It is used most often when the need is for above ground rotary heads. It is manually activated and manually disconnected. It is made of brass on galvanized pipe and will probably last forever. (See Figs. 1-28 through 1-36.)

Controllers

Controllers are the devices that you use to operate the main valve and the remote-control valves within the system design. They regulate

Fig. 1-28. The main city valve often is housed in a meter box in your front lawn area. Some older neighborhoods do not have boxes. The valves are just below the surface of the ground, usually about two feet in depth. Depending upon city code requirements, it might or might not have a turn handle. Some cities require the use of a special key for operation. Photograph courtesy of James Hardie Irrigation.

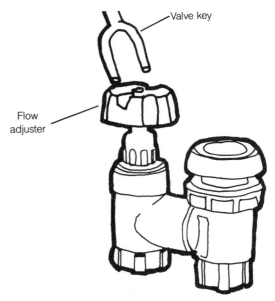

Fig. 1-29. The manual control valve for a sprinkler circuit has a key to adjust the flow of water within the system. Information courtesy of James Hardie Irrigation.

Fig. 1-30. The circuit valves are simple units that adjust the flow of water to the various sections of your landscape. These automatic units show the wires which lead to the system timer. Photograph courtesy of James Hardie Irrigation.

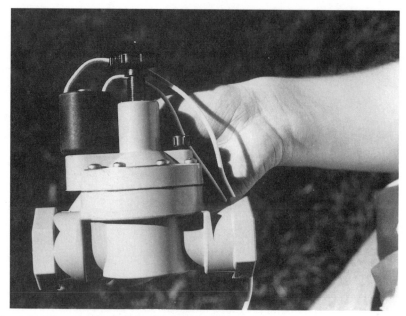

Fig. 1-31. The circuit valves for the different parts of your system are small and easy to install in just a few minutes.

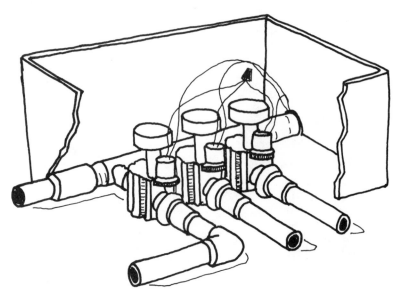

Fig. 1-32. Cluster automatic valves together for convenience whenever possible. You can place them within your garage or basement if desired. The cluster has a hand-operated shutoff (main control) valve. Information courtesy of James Hardie Irrigation.

Fig. 1-33A and B. Some of the larger systems require a large box to protect the clusters of valves (A). For small residential programs, you can use the smaller boxes to protect the valves (B).

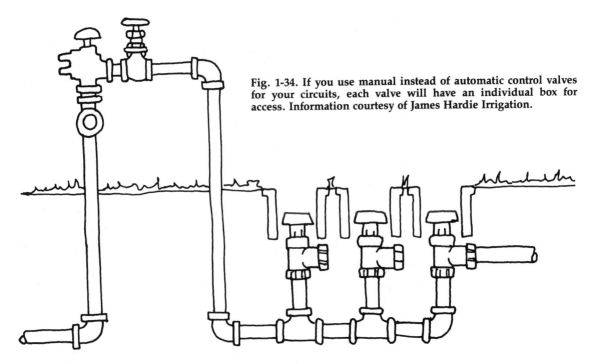

Fig. 1-34. If you use manual instead of automatic control valves for your circuits, each valve will have an individual box for access. Information courtesy of James Hardie Irrigation.

the power to the valves in electricity or hydraulic pressure. For the home lawn sprinkler system, electricity is the best form of power.

The electric controller operates mostly from a standard 115 volt AC power source. You actually can plug the unit into a standard plug found in most homes today. Usually you have circuits for the master control valve and ones for the remote valves. Timers within these units allow

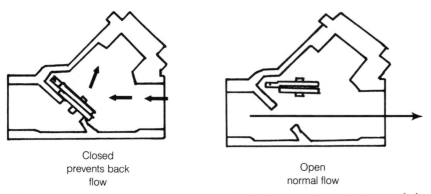

Closed
prevents back
flow

Open
normal flow

Fig. 1-35. The basic operation of this valve is simple, but very important to your irrigation system.

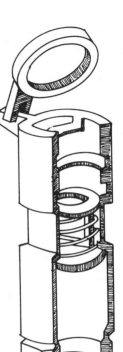

Fig. 1-36. The quick coupling valve is activated when the sprinkler unit is inserted into the valve socket.

Fig. 1-37. This program unit uses a touch control for operating an automatic system. Photograph courtesy of James Hardie Irrigation.

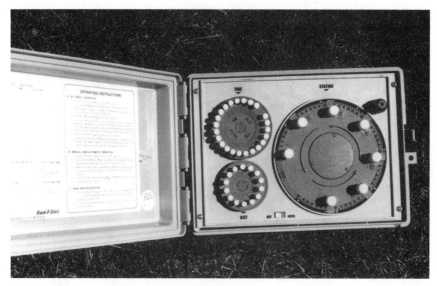

Fig. 1-38. This standard clock unit operates up to seven sprinkler circuits during a 24 hour period.

you to set the operation of your system cycles to your needs, day or night. (See Figs. 1-37 through 1-40.)

Pipe

The term *pipe* applies to any hollow tubing (flexible or rigid) that carries water within a home sprinkler irrigation system. The majority of pipe within your system will range in size up to one inch. Larger pipe probably will decrease the efficiency of your system.

Some general piping terminology important to your system design is:

O.D.—the actual diameter of a piece of pipe measured straight across the open end of the widest point to the outside of the walls of the pipe. (See Figs. 1-41 through 1-46 and Table 1-5 and 1-6.)

Table 1-5. Pipe Selection.

When selecting the type of pipe to use for your system, consider the following factors as a guideline:

- *Flow Characteristics*—how much friction loss will each pipe material have?
- *Pipe Strength*—what is the burst pressure rating of the pipe?
- *Life Expectancy*—how long will it last?
- *Soil Type*—the harder the soil type, the more expensive it is.
- *Cost*—compare the costs of additional materials.

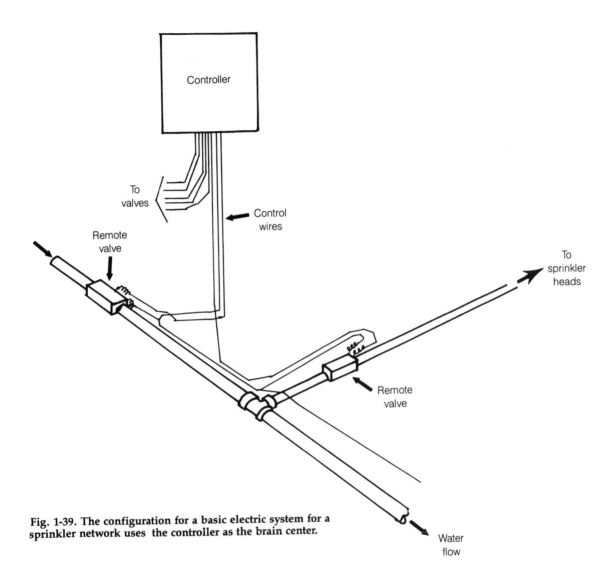

Fig. 1-39. The configuration for a basic electric system for a sprinkler network uses the controller as the brain center.

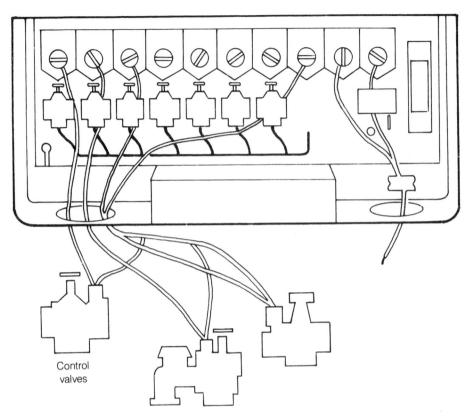

Control
valves

Fig. 1-40. The wiring connectors within the controller are easy to install and maintain. Information courtesy of James Hardie Irrigation.

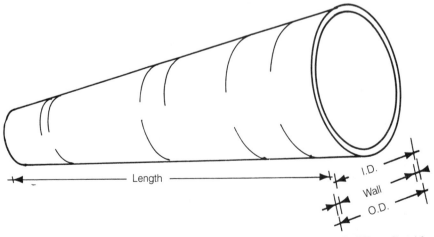

I.D.

Wall

O.D.

Length

Fig. 1-41. The standard pipe terms are: ID = Insider Diameter and, OD = Outside Diameter.

Fig. 1-42. PVC pipe is a standard material widely available in hardware and building supply stores.

Fig. 1-43. The roll of polypipe is a common sight on most projects. It is light weight and is used to connect the individual heads to the valve cluster stations.

**Table 1-6. The Advantages and Disadvantages
of the Most Commonly Used Pipe Materials.**

Plastic Pipe

- Does not corrode or scale under most weather conditions.
- Is not subject to chemical damage.
- Has various pressure ratings.
- Is subject to expansion and contraction from temperature fluctuations.
- Is low cost.
- Is easy to install.

Polyethylene Pipe

- Flexible, available in coils.
- Low strength.
- Various pressure ratings.
- Expands in heat.
- Low cost.

PVC (poly-vinyl-chloride pipe)

- Available in various pressure ratings.
- Outside diameter is constant.
- High strength.
- Not readily affected by temperature.
- Requires solvent to weld joints.

Information courtesy of Rainbird Sales, Inc.

Fig. 1-44. Various sizes of polypipe are available for your use. On the left are those used for high pressure systems. On the right are the smaller types used for drip systems. Photograph courtesy of James Hardie Irrigation.

Fig. 1-45. Use the basic PVC "elbow" and "T" joints to connect the various pieces of polypipe together.

Fig. 1-46. A simple screwdriver and ring clamp are all that you need to connect the PVC joints to a polypipe section.

2

Designing Your System

EVALUATING YOUR PROPERTY IS THE FIRST STEP IN DESIGNING YOUR SPRIN-
kler system. A fundamental relationship exists between the sprinkler
system you desire for your lawn and the existing soil conditions on your
property. Poor soils will prevent the most sophisticated system from
functioning properly. An analysis of your soil conditions is an important
step in the predesign process.

The soil surrounding your sprinkler system is important for a number of reasons. It must support plant growth; it must be easily workable
during installation; and, most of all, it must hold enough water for plants
to grow and be an attractive addition to your landscape.

In general, the water-holding capacity of the soil on your property
will determine the eventual success or failure of your sprinkler system.
Too much water in the soil will assist the formation of fungus growth
which kills many popular ornamental lawn grasses. Not enough water
will retard plant growth and prevent the bright green colors of attractive
lawns. (See Figs. 2-1 through 2-3.)

Water-holding capacities are related specifically to the size of the particles of soil. The coarser the soil, the lower water-holding capacity it has.
Fine-textured soils have a low water intake rate, but hold the water
longer. The ideal soil will have a balance between water intake and water-
holding capacity.

The United States Department of Agriculture has identified six basic
soil types which might apply to your property. These soil types are:

1. *Sand*—loose, single-grained material. You can see and feel the individual grains. Pure sand properties will not support enough plant growth to justify a sprinkler system. The water might drain away too fast.
2. *Sandy Loam*—contains mostly sand but has enough silt and clay to make it support plant growth. You could use a sprinkler system in this soil condition. It will hold enough water.
3. *Loam*—a soil type having a mixture of the different grades of sand, silt, and clay in such proportions that the characteristics of no one type predominates. A system probably would function

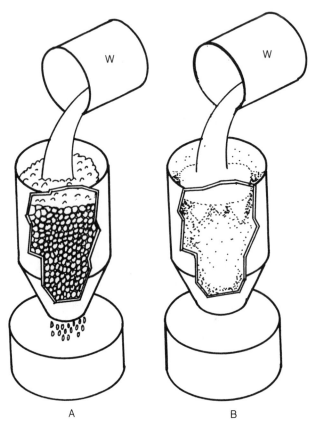

A   B

Fig. 2-1. The size of the soil particles in your lawn will affect the ability of the soil to hold water. As water is held by the soil, the moisture becomes available for the grasses and plants. Coarse soils (A) have a high water intake rate but a low water-holding capacity. Fine soils (B) have a low water intake rate but a high water holding capacity. Information courtesy of Irrigation System's design manual; Buckner Irrigation Systems.

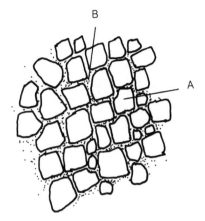

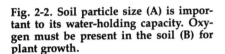

Fig. 2-2. Soil particle size (A) is important to its water-holding capacity. Oxygen must be present in the soil (B) for plant growth.

quite well in this soil. This soil has good balance of intake and holding characteristics.

4. *Silt Loam*—a soil having a moderate amount of fine grades of sand and a small amount of clay. A sprinkler system might have problems with this soil type. It might not drain fast enough for some landscape plants.

5. *Clay Loam*—a fine-textured soil which holds moisture to the point where you can knead it in your hand. A sprinkler system in this

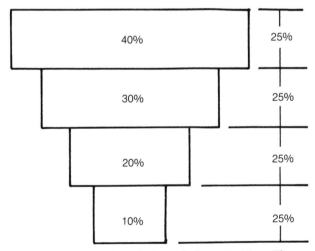

Fig. 2-3. Water absorption by plants is through the root system. The amount of water the plants absorb is related to the total depth of the roots. Approximately 40 percent of the moisture plants need is taken in within the first 25 percent. During times of water shortages when you must shorten sprinkler operations, it is possible to deliver up to 70 percent of needed plant moisture through the first 50 percent of root depth. Information courtesy of USDA, Soil Conservation Service.

soil could create problems for your plants. This type soil holds excessive amounts of water.

6. *Clay*—a fine-textured soil that usually forms hard lumps or clods and restricts water movement. A sprinkler system is not recommended for this type of soil condition. Clay soil holds too much water.

SOIL FACTORS AND PLANT GROWTH

Soil will influence the growth of plants in your irrigated landscape by the following factors:

- Supporting and anchoring the plants.
- Holding and supplying essential nutrients.
- Holding and supplying essential water.
- Holding and supplying essential oxygen.
- Reducing growth inhibiting salts.

The physical properties of the soil on your site influences each of these factors. Each of the specific properties relates to the capabilities of the soil in supporting a lawn sprinkler system.

For example, soil *texture* indicates the size of the soil particles and its ability to intake and hold moisture for your landscape plants. The USDA classifies soil particles by size as follows:

Type	Diameter (MM)
Very coarse sand	2.00—1.00
Coarse sand	1.00—0.50
Medium sand	0.50—0.25
Fine sand	0.25—0.10
Very fine sand	0.10—0.05
Silt	0.05—0.002
Clay	Less than 0.002

(You can change the texture of the soil by adding soil separates such as sand to clay soils or vice versa.)

The quality of water that you can hold in a form available for plants is influenced by the quantity of clay and organic matter in the specific soil. The amount of water held within each soil type is as follows:

Soil Texture	Type	Inches/Foot
Coarse	Sand	0.50
Fine	Sand	0.75
Loamy	Sand	1.00
Fine	Sandy loam	1.25—1.50
Silt	Loam	1.75—2.00
Silty	Clay loam	2.00
Clay	Loam	2.00—2.25

To test your soil by its feel, dig a small hole equal to the depth of the roots of your lawn grass. If your house is new and no grass exists, dig the hole approximately twelve inches deep. Take a handful of soil and compare the size of the particles with the previous chart. To estimate moisture content, use the following to compare the feel and appearance of several samples taken from various parts of your property:

Test No. 1
Soil moisture deficiency—0 percent

Coarse texture—Upon squeezing the soil, no free water appears in your hand. A moist outline of the soil ball might, however, be left in your hand.

Moderately coarse texture—Upon squeezing the soil, no free water appears in your hand, but a wet outline of a ball might be left in your hand.

Medium texture—Upon squeezing the soil, no free water appears in your hand, but the wet outline of a ball might be left in your hand.

Fine texture—Upon squeezing the soil, no free water appears in your hand, but the wet outline of a ball might be left in your hand.

Test No. 2
Soil moisture deficiency—0 percent to 25 percent

Coarse texture—The soil tends to stick together slightly. Sometimes the soil forms a very weak ball under pressure.

Moderately coarse texture—The soil forms a weak ball, breaks easily, and will not stick.

Medium texture—The soil forms a ball, is very pliable, and sticks readily.

Fine texture—The soil easily ribbons out between fingers and has a slick feeling.

Test No. 3
Soil moisture deficiency—25 percent to 50 percent

Coarse texture—The soil appears to be dry and will not form a ball with pressure.

Moderately coarse texture—The soil tends to ball under pressure, but seldom holds together.

Medium texture—The soil forms a ball and will sometimes stick slightly with pressure.

Fine texture—The soil forms a ball and ribbons out between the thumb and the forefinger.

Test No. 4

Soil moisture deficiency—50 percent to 75 percent

Coarse texture—The soil appears to be dry and will not form a ball with pressure.

Moderately coarse texture—The soil appears to be dry and will not form a ball.

Medium texture—The soil is somewhat crumbly but holds together from pressure.

Fine texture—The soil is somewhat pliable. It will ball under pressure.

Text No. 5

Soil moisture deficiency—75 percent to 100 percent

Coarse texture—The soil is dry, loose, single-grained and flows through your fingers.

Moderately coarse texture—The soil is dry and loose. It flows through your fingers.

Medium texture—The soil is powdery, dry, and slightly crusted, but it is broken down easily into a powdery condition.

Fine texture—The soil is hard, baked, and cracked. It sometimes crumbs on the surface.

Professionals in the irrigation industry have used this field test technique for soil moisture for many years. It provides sufficient accuracy for determining the soil moisture content that exists for your landscape.

If you find that the existing moisture capability is low, your design might require a high capacity system. If you find that the existing moisture capability is high, a low capacity system might fit your needs best.

You should test your site and record the findings. Remember, only general soil capabilities near the root zone of the plants is important.

Factors that will influence existing soil moisture and also will relate to the design of your system are as follows:

• The amount of available sunlight on the various parts of your property.

- The temperatures during the growing seasons.
- The atmosphere vapor pressures.
- The various directions and velocities of seasonal winds.
- The natural supply (rainfall) of soil moisture.

The ability of the soil to take in water during the time your system is running is called the *infiltration rate*. The conditions on the surface of your lawn and the physical characteristics of the soil govern this rate. The initial infiltration rate is very high and then diminishes rapidly. If your system runs too long, you will waste water and cause surface runoff. You must run your system fewer hours or increase the infiltration rate.

The factors that will affect infiltration rate are as follows:

- The slope of your property. Severe slopes will reduce the rate.
- Plant cover. Lawn thatch will impede infiltration severely.
- Soil conditions. Poor texture and compacted soil will prevent infiltration.
- Time. Running a system for too short a time period might promote water loss by evaporation before it reaches the root systems.
- Existing soil moisture. If adequate moisture already exists, do not water. Wait for the time when moisture is needed.

You can improve the infiltration rate by the following:

- Remove lawn thatch each year to allow more water through to the root systems of your plants.
- Aerate the lawn to provide better soil structure.
- Add soil amendments to provide a better texture.
- Water more frequently for shorter time periods.

Since you desire a sprinkler system for your home, the relationship between soils, moisture, and the plants on your property cannot be over emphasized. How plants use the water you will provide is also important.

The primary method of water absorption by plants is through the roots. Surface roots absorb the water first and then the root hairs absorb it at successfully greater depths. The amount of water available to plants depends upon the depth of the roots. Most lawn grasses have shallow roots, requiring more water for growth cycles.

The factors which affect water absorption by the root systems of plants are:

- Amount of water available in the soil.
- The temperature of the soil.
- Aeration of the soil.
- The health of the root system.
- The type of plant.

The specific water requirements for your plants and property will be affected by the seasonal moisture patterns for your region, the groundwater table for your area, and the application efficiency of the system you will design and install. Generally, to accommodate the requirements of the plants, the soils, and the watering system, it is best to achieve a stable soil base.

The *structure* of the soil relates to the arrangement of the soil particles such as sand, clay, and organic matter. Structure will influence the rate of water and air movement within the soil. To change the structure of your soil, you need only to aerate or till to the proper planting depth.

The *temperature* of the soil is important for proper plant growth. Soils that have a tendency to hold moisture will become warmer and cooler more slowly than drier ones. This temperature promotes the proper exchange of plant nutrients, and allows a sprinkler system to perform efficiently.

The ideal percent of soil particles and materials as recommended by most irrigation companies is as follows:

- 45 percent—mineral matter.
- 5 percent—organic matter.
- 25 percent—moisture.
- 25 percent—air.

This balanced soil is ideal for plant growth and allows the sprinkler system to maintain the conditions necessary for a successful landscape. If your existing soil is not adequate for a balanced relationship between water and plants, you might need to add materials to create a more suitable soil condition. Most soil amendments are available readily at a local nursery or garden center. Most local offices of the United States Soil Conservation Service offer soil-testing services.

THE SLOPE OF YOUR PROPERTY

The second most important predesign factor is slope. Since most yards are flat, slope will not be a critical issue to consider. However, if the slope of your property exceeds 10 percent, the water available for plant

Fig. 2-4. Use a string and heavy weight to estimate the slope of your yard. Place the point of the string at the highest point on your property. Walk down the slope to a convenient location and hold the string level. Let the weight tied to the end drop to the ground, so the angle you are holding forms 90 degrees. The "triangle" created by the string and yard will help you determine an approximate percentage of slope.

growth will be less, due to excessive surface runoff. The illustration below indicates a simple method for determining your slope. If your property has a slope greater than 10 percent you might wish to reconsider your decision to install a sprinkler system. (See Figs. 2-4 through 2-5.)

To summarize your soil, slope, and water relationships, use the following chart to determine the conditions of your property. (See Table 2-1.)

Table 2-1. Average Water Application Rates (Ranges)
for Soils/Slopes (Inches/Hour).

Soil Type	0% Slope	10% Slope
Sandy loam	1.5-1.9	.9-1. 1
Silty loam	.9-1.1	.5- .7
Clay	.1- .3	.09- .11

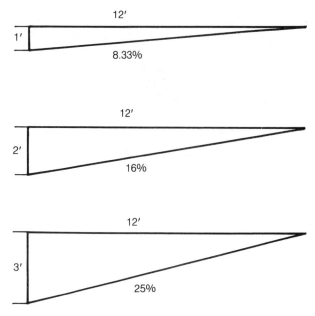

Fig. 2-5. Compare your triangle to one of these to determine your approximate percentage of slope.

AUTOMATIC OR MANUAL HIGH-PRESSURE SYSTEM

You should follow two important steps in designing your sprinkler system. Each step has a number of tasks that, when completed, will provide you with the basic data necessary for completing your system design. The first is the *information gathering step* which leads to the *layout and drawing step*. Both are important for a successful system.

Information Gathering Step

Measuring Your Property's Water Capacity. *Water capacity*, measured in gallons per minute (gpm), is the maximum flow of water that can be delivered to your sprinkler system. To determine gpm, locate your water meter and note its size. Most meters are $5/8$, $3/4$, or 1 inch. The size often is stamped on the side of the meter.

If you cannot locate your meter, call your local water service company. They will be able to give you most of the information you need to start the design process, such as:

- The size and location of your water meter.
- The static water pressure in your home.

• Local codes and permits concerning the installation of underground sprinkler systems.

Next, measure the diameter of the service line leaving the meter. This line goes from the meter to your home. Measure this pipe immediately after the meter. If your property has been developed recently, your water service company probably will have this information.

To measure the pipe diameter, wrap a string around the pipe. Do this about four to six inches away from the meter. If this service line is copper or galvanized pipe, check the length of your string against the following chart to determine the pipe size.

If your water service company does not know the static water pressure, you must measure it as follows:

• Turn off all water.
• Attach a pressure gauge to an outside faucet and turn the faucet on.
• Read the number indicated on the dial and write it down.

If your water is supplied by a pump, call your pump service company. They will know the flow rate (gpm) and pressure (psi). If you have a pressure tank, contact a local plumber or water engineer to obtain this information. (See the following two charts and Fig. 2-6.)

Check Local Codes.

Be sure you check the local codes and permit requirements concerning the installation of underground sprinkler systems. Code restrictions might influence (1) pipe material, (2) type and location of back-flow preventer, (3) method of tie-in to the water main, and (4) other procedures and materials of construction. (Information adapted from "Planning and Installation Guide," courtesy of the TORO Company.)

Measuring the Diameter of Your Service Line.

Measure the length of the pipe after the meter. If you don't have a meter, measure the pipe running from the street into your home. To determine pipe diameter, wrap a string around the pipe, measure the length of the string circling the pipe, and check the diameter with the chart below.

Length of String	$2^3/_4$"	$3^1/_4$"	$3^1/_2$"	4"	$4^3/_8$"	5"
Size of Copper Line	$3/_4$"		1"		$1^1/_4$"	
Size of Galvanized Line		$3/_4$"		1"		

(Information adapted from "Planning and Installation Guide," courtesy of The TORO Company.)

Fig. 2-6. After obtaining a pressure gauge, attach it to an outside faucet. Turn off all running water inside and outside of your property. Turn on the faucet with the gauge attached and record the reading on the gauge. This is your static water pressure. Photograph courtesy of James Hardie Irrigation.

Based upon the field information you have collected for the size of your meter, the diameter of your service line, and your static water pressure, use the following service line chart to determine your water capacity.

Variations will exist from subdivision to subdivision through the country. If your home is in a new neighborhood, water pressures might be greater now than in the planned future. You should contact your local water authority to obtain information on future water availability.

This *water capacity* information is especially important if you wish to develop an automatic or manual, high-pressure irrigation system. You must control the gpm and psi uniformly if your system is to function properly. (See Appendix A for the Water Supply Comparison Chart.)

Measuring Your Property. Although many residential properties have existing layout plans, it is necessary that you develop a new plot plan for more accurate planning of your system. Begin with a free hand sketch of your property using the extension of building walls method of measurement. Locate all of the major features of your property based upon this technique, using the corners of your house as reference points. (See Figs. 2-7 and 2-8.)

It is best to locate all permanent features on your plan. Although you can move shrubs easily, consider them permanent features. Indicate all individual shrubs, planting beds, trees, retaining walls, fences, and posts. If you have a new property, you should design your landscape plan and then design your sprinkler system.

In addition to your landscape features, note the following important elements on your plot plan:

1. Low window locations. If you have a basement or window that is close to the ground, note these on the plan. You do not want to spray these features with water.
2. Adjacent property features. As residential lots become smaller, it is important for you to be aware of your neighbor's property. You do not want to water parts of your neighbor's lawn or landscape, nor do you want to spray water on your neighbor's driveway or patio. You could be held liable for any damage or accident resulting in this unwanted watering.
3. City water supply. Note this feature on the plan so you can indicate the starting point for your system design.
4. A convenient location for your controls if you are developing an automatic system.
5. True north. Since prevailing winds will be an important factor, use a compass to locate true north.

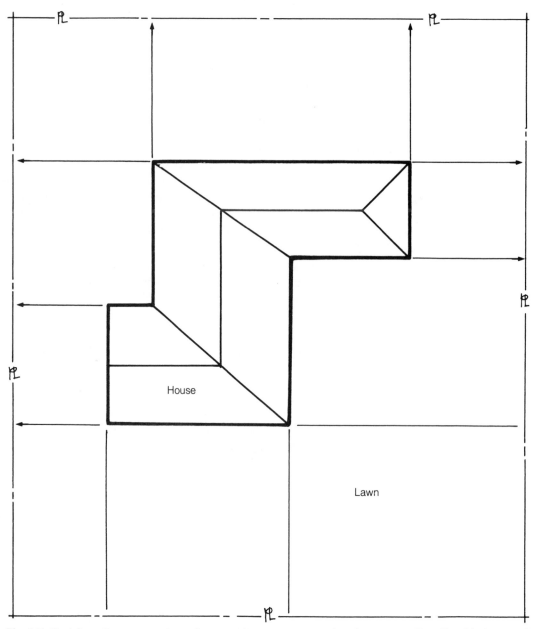

Fig. 2-7. Start from the corners of your house and measure outward to the property line. Do this from each corner until you have determined the accurate shape of your landscape area.

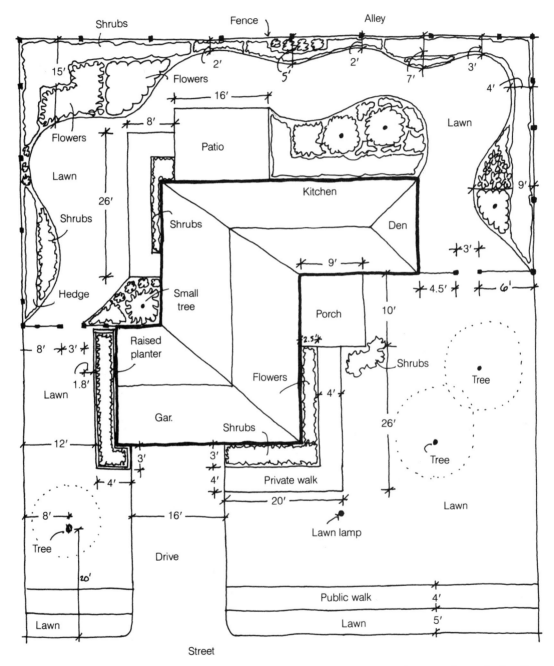

Fig. 2-8. Once you locate your property lines, make an inventory of your landscape and note the location of the walks, drive, trees, and shrub areas. Also note any obstacle you feel might interfere with the delivery of water from the sprinkler heads.

For the plant material on your property, it is important for you to remember the following: (See Figs. 2-9 through 2-14.)

1. The size and height of your shrubs and shrub areas. For individual shrubs, you should note heights above four feet. Shrub sprinkler heads above this height will not perform properly. Shrub masses might restrict the use of spray heads altogether. Bubbler heads might be necessary for these plantings.
2. Specialty planting areas. Some plants, such as roses, should not have their foliage wet. If you have, or desire, these types of plantings, spray or stream heads will not be practical. If these specialty planting areas are extensive enough, they might require a separate circuit from the lawn area.
3. Trees with low-hanging branches. These features, too, will obstruct the delivery of water to areas of your lawn. For these trees, note the edge of the branches and mark them on your plan.
4. Small trees grow into big trees. Although the trees in the lawn might be small now, they will grow larger. Plan your system for the future, not for the present.

Fig. 2-9. Be sure to measure the approximate location of each existing or proposed planting bed. The distance from the house to the edge of the groundcover is measured here.

A

B

Fig. 2-10 A & B. The best method for noting trees on your plan is to measure their location from the corner of the house.

Fig. 2-11. Groundcover masses next to walks can be measured to a depth from the existing walk.

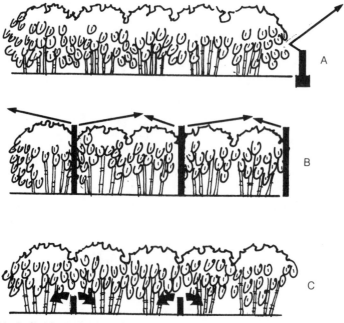

Fig. 2-12. Individual shrubs and shrub masses might require separate heads for proper watering. Rotary pop-up (A) often delivers water only to the outer portion of the plants. Shrub spray heads often water only the top of the plants. A low-height bubble head (C) will reach the ground and provide more water to the plants.

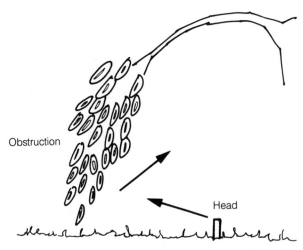

Fig. 2-13. Some tree varieties have branches that hang low to the ground and obstruct spray patterns.

Layout and Design Step

The Plot Plan. Now that you have the basic information for your property measured, recorded, and sketched onto a piece of paper, it is necessary to make a scaled drawing of your lot.

First, obtain a sheet of grid paper, approximately 11 inches × 17 inches in size. Each grid on this sheet will represent one foot of distance on the ground. This method is easy and convenient for transferring your sketch data to a scaled drawing.

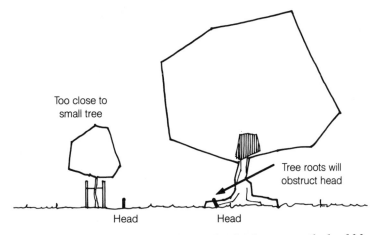

Fig. 2-14. This new tree might be small now, but its future growth should be your planning factor.

17"

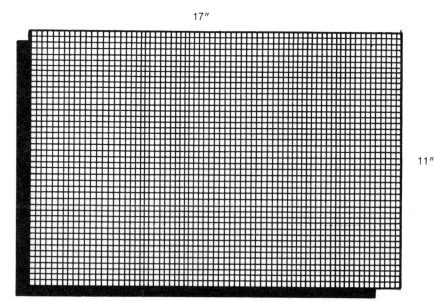

11"

Fig. 2-15. For developing your irrigation plan, use a 11" × 17" sheet of grid paper. This is a convenient size for working on a small table or checking your work outside.

Next, divide your yard into as many rectangular or square zones as possible. This procedure will help with the location of the heads. Now you are ready to begin the final design task.

Designing Your Automatic System. The items you must consider now include sprinkler head selection and placement, water supply and circuiting, and pipe sizing and routing. (See Figs. 2-15 and 2-16.)

The selection of a particular sprinkler head depends upon the following:

- The size and shape of your lawn area.
- The number and types of obstructions on your property.
- Availability of water and working pressure.
- Soil type.
- Special plantings.

The spacing of the heads you select will depend upon the following:

- Prevailing winds.
- Diameter of the sprinkler pattern.
- The working pressure of the head.
- Type of plant material being watered.

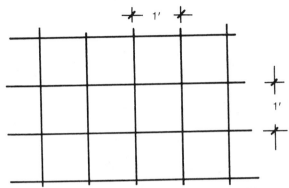

Fig. 2-16. Select a grid page where the squares of the grid will represent one foot of ground distance. This will make your measuring efforts much easier.

For the average residential landscape, most of the sprinkler heads sold through local hardware stores and building supply dealers are more than adequate for your needs. Sophisticated control boxes and intricate piping systems are becoming a thing of the past. New design technologies have allowed sprinkler heads to become more efficient in delivering water to your landscape. High impact, sturdy, plastic heads have replaced heavy brass heads. Flexible hoses have replaced ridged pipe networks. You can use a simple garden shovel for trenching where once a massive machine was required.

As we discussed in chapter 1, you must consider two types of sprinkler heads—the spray head and the rotary head.

You can use the spray head around small turf areas or irregularly-shaped landscapes where water application rates can vary. They operate at a relatively low pressure (ranging from 15 to 30 psi), and you should restrict them to areas smaller than 36 feet in radius. If you require precise watering into delicate areas of your lawn, the spray head will fit requirements.

A rotary head, on the other hand, operates at a higher pressure (ranging from 30 to 70 psi). For larger expanses of lawn and landscape, they are most economical. Because of their water-delivery range of up to 90 feet, you will need fewer heads in the system. If your landscape can tolerate a broad application of water without damaging your plants, they will meet your requirements. (See Figs. 2-17 through 2-19.)

An important point to remember about the use of sprinkler heads is that you should never mix them on a single circuit. Spray heads and rotary heads require different operating pressures for peak efficiency. When you mix the heads on a single circuit, the only efficient head is the one nearest to the water source.

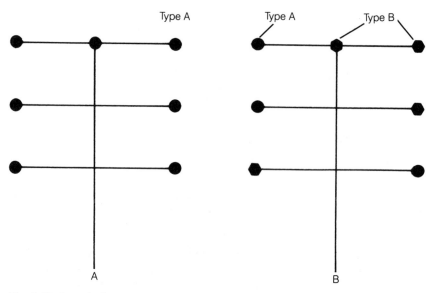

Fig. 2-17. A typical sprinkler circuit should contain only one type of sprinkler head (as shown in A).

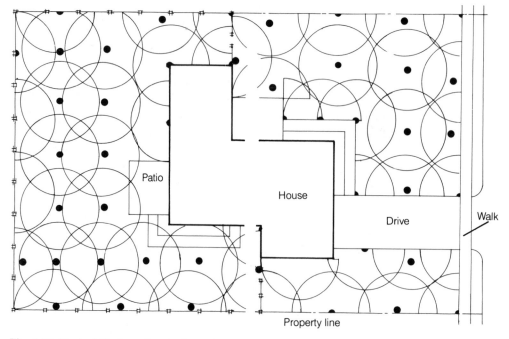

Fig. 2-18. Typical Design—Square Layout

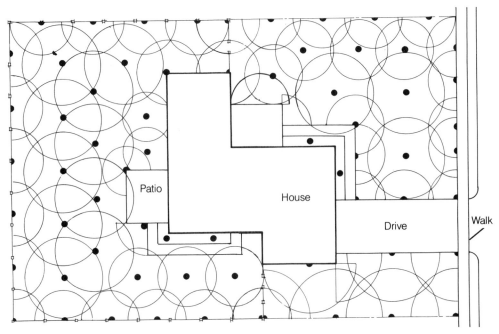

Fig. 2-19. Typical Design—Triangular Layout

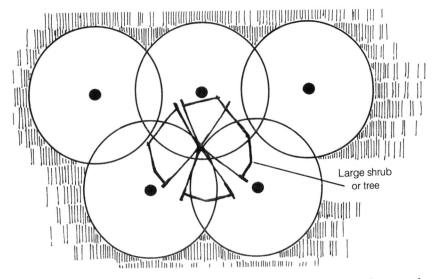

Fig. 2-20. Large shrubs or small ornamental trees should be placed in between the heads and away from the piping network. The coverage patterns will be able to maintain moisture to the lawn area. Design courtesy of Rain Bird Sales, Inc.

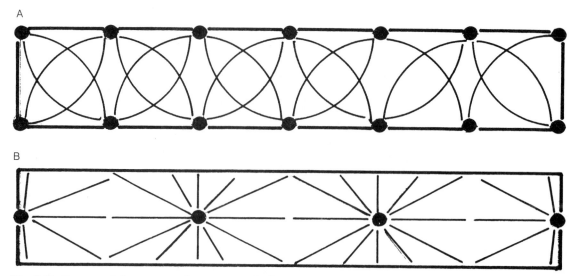

Fig. 2-21. You can attain narrow strip coverage which often borders a drive or walk by using two-head arrangements. (A) Two rows of half-circle heads. (B) Center strip heads spraying in two directions. Design courtesy of Rain Bird Sales, Inc.

Following are helpful hints for circuit design (side bar):

- Do not mix sprinkler types within a single circuit.
- Place lawn sprinklers and shrub sprinklers on separate circuits.
- Do not mix low gallonage sprinklers and standard gallonage sprinklers.
- Place shaded area sprinklers and sunny area sprinklers on separate circuits.
- Each circuit should have near equal pressure capacity.

Information courtesy of "Planning and Installation Guide," The TORO Company.

Most high-pressure sprinkler heads are manufactured for specific coverage capacity, minimum/maximum spacing needs, and flow requirements. Never assume just any sprinkler head will meet your needs. Make certain that your design will accommodate the capabilities of the heads you select. (See Figs. 2-20 and 2-21.)

Two basic spacing patterns are used to locate high-pressure sprinkler heads—square spacing and triangular spacing. Both patterns adequately deliver the water to your lawn and usually are selected based upon the following:

- The shape of your property.
- The open areas to be watered.
- The types of obstructions.
- The amount of water and the working pressure.
- The characteristics of the water from the heads (stream or spray).
- The amount of anticipated winds.
- Special planting areas.

Overlapping of coverage areas in either pattern is not only desirable, but required. Water loses its force as it leaves the head and is subject to distortion at the edges of the coverage circle. On the outer edges, you should note critical points and adjust sprinkler heads to deliver the proper amounts of water. Each manufacturer has suggested performance standards for the heads they sell.

With square spacing, you must locate heads at each of four corners formed by the square. For triangular spacing, locate heads at each of the three points formed by the triangle. Triangular spacing has proven to be most economical for residential landscapes.

Standard spacing between typical heads in the triangular configuration is 20 feet. If the available pressure is low, you can reduce spacing to 15 feet if necessary. A basic spacing of less than 15 feet is not advisable. If your design results in a closer spacing, you might need to redesign your system with fewer, more efficient heads. Other spacing arrangements for flower beds, lost corners, shrubs, tree groupings, and those odd-sized areas in your landscape are illustrated in Figs. 2-22 through 2-43.

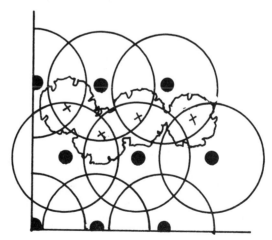

Fig. 2-22. You can water a group of trees or large shrubs from outside heads. Design courtesy of Buckner Irrigation.

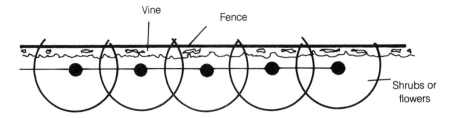

Fig. 2-23. You can water a vine or fence from shrub heads in the foreground. Design courtesy of Buckner Irrigation.

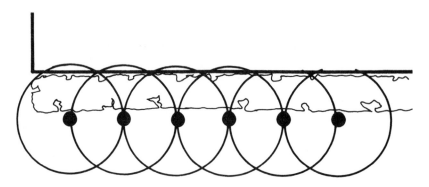

Fig. 2-24. You can water low hedges against a wall by heads in front that also can water the lawn areas. Design courtesy of Buckner Irrigation.

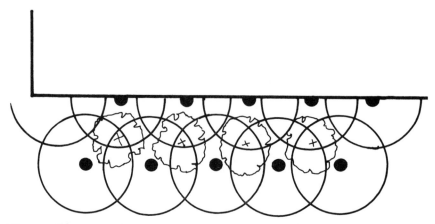

Fig. 2-25. You can water open shrub plantings by spray heads in front and behind the shrubs. Design courtesy of Buckner Irrigation.

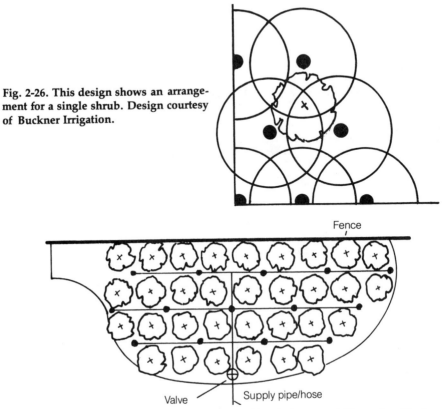

Fig. 2-26. This design shows an arrangement for a single shrub. Design courtesy
of Buckner Irrigation.

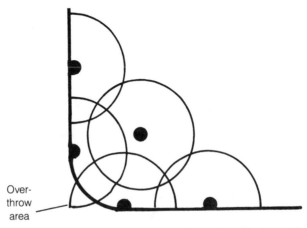

Fence

Valve   Supply pipe/hose

Fig. 2-27. This design shows an arrangement of heads for a vegetable garden. Design
courtesy of Buckner Irrigation.

Over-
throw
area

Fig. 2-28. A head arrangement for a corner will require adjustment to prevent an
overthrow area. Design courtesy of Rain Bird Sales, Inc.

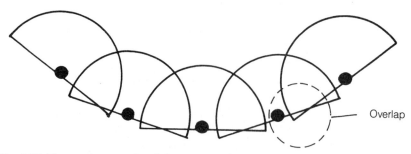

Fig. 2-29. You must space a head arrangement for an outside curve properly to allow an overlap for proper coverage. Design courtesy of Rain Bird Sales, Inc.

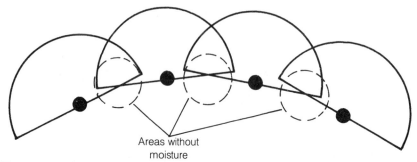

Fig. 2-30. Incorrect spacing for an outside curve will create areas without moisture. Design courtesy of Rain Bird Sales, Inc.

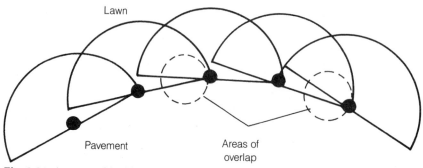

Fig. 2-31. A reversed inside curve also requires an overlap area for moisture control. Design courtesy of Buckner Irrigation.

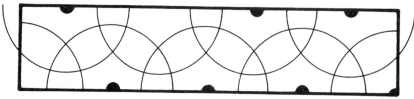

Fig. 2-32. You can water a flower bed with half-circle heads arranged on the edges of the planting area. Design courtesy of Buckner Irrigation.

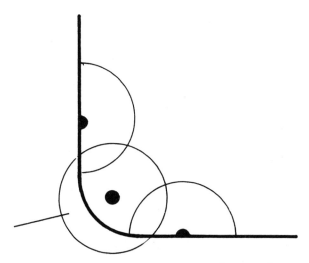

Fig. 2-33. Corner arrangements for round corners may have overthrow areas. Design courtesy of Buckner Irrigation.

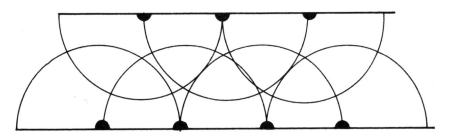

Fig. 2-34. You can cover narrow areas between buildings with half-circle heads. Design courtesy of Buckner Irrigation.

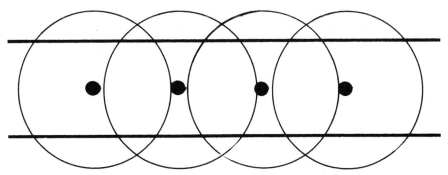

Fig. 2-35. This design shows an alternative arrangement for a narrow strip of landscape. Design courtesy of Buckner Irrigation.

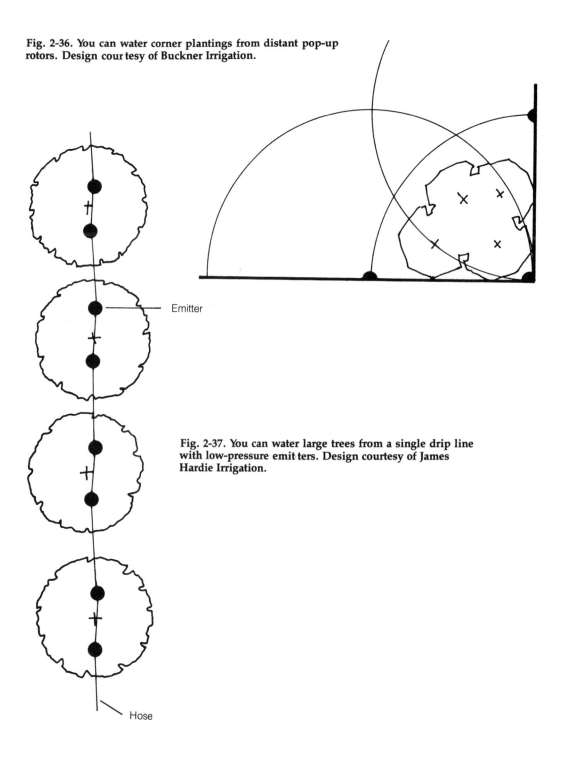

Fig. 2-36. You can water corner plantings from distant pop-up rotors. Design courtesy of Buckner Irrigation.

Emitter

Fig. 2-37. You can water large trees from a single drip line with low-pressure emitters. Design courtesy of James Hardie Irrigation.

Hose

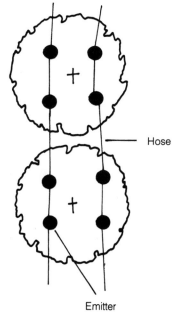

Hose

Emitter

Fig. 2-38. Use two lateral drip lines to water medium-size trees. Design courtesy of James Hardie Irrigation.

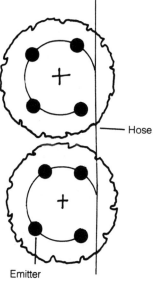

Hose

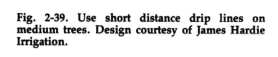

Emitter

Fig. 2-39. Use short distance drip lines on medium trees. Design courtesy of James Hardie Irrigation.

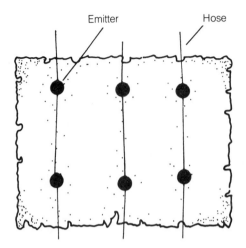

Fig. 2-40. You can apply low pressure drip lines to groundcover areas. Design courtesy of James Hardie Irrigation.

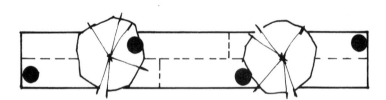

Fig. 2-41. You can water narrow lawn areas which have trees with heads that have a narrow radius of throw. This will prevent the trees from becoming obstructions. Illustration courtesy of James Hardie Irrigation.

Fig. 2-42. You can water some very small areas by a single, centered head. Illustration courtesy of James Hardie Irrigation.

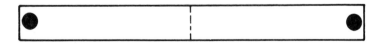

Fig. 2-43. Heads at each end of a long narrow strip of lawn will provide the needed moisture. Illustration courtesy of James Hardie Irrigation.

Problems you might wish to avoid in your layout are shown in Figs. 2-44 through 2-47.

Water Supply and Circuiting. From your field notes taken on water supply and available pressure, you can begin to establish the different

Fig. 2-44. This rotary pop-up is too close to this high-traffic corner. Not only will the grass not grow, but the potential damage to the head is also great.

Fig. 2-45. This stationary spray head is located too close to this high-traffic corner. It eventually will be stepped on and damaged, making it a trouble spot for this system.

Fig. 2-46. This stationary head, although located in a groundcover area, could prove hazardous if someone was to fall on it.

circuits you will have in your system. Each portion of your landscape might have a separate circuit, or zone, for peak operating efficiency.

A *circuit* is a specific group of heads that operate together off of a common valve. The system timer will operate this circuit independently from the other circuits. The total operating pressure for each circuit, therefore, cannot exceed the total operating pressure for your property.

For example, the open lawn area near the patio, in the design example, will be covered best by rotary heads. These heads will be on an individual circuit and an independent valve grouped with other valves in a valve box will control them. The total system divided into appropriate circuits is shown in Fig. 2-51.

The capacity for each circuit is determined by the type and number of heads you have selected, which has been set by the manufacturer. For convenience, make a note of the gpm and pressure requirement for each head on the circuit. Total these requirements and check the totals against the available pressure. (See Figs. 2-48 through 2-50 and Tables 2-2 and 2-3.) Within the landscaped area in Fig. 2-50, there are six heads. Four are rated by their manufacturer at 1.28 gpm and two are rated at 2.58

Fig. 2-47. Water from the sprinkler heads have stained this wooden fence. This condition will shorten the life of an attractive garden feature.

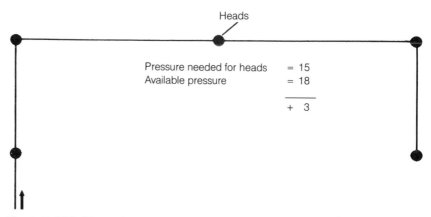

Heads

Pressure needed for heads = 15
Available pressure = 18

+ 3

Fig. 2-48. This illustration shows a good design for circuit calculation.

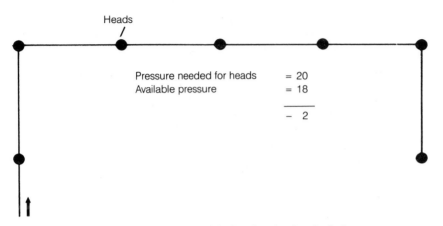

Fig. 2-49. This illustration shows a poor design for circuit calculation.

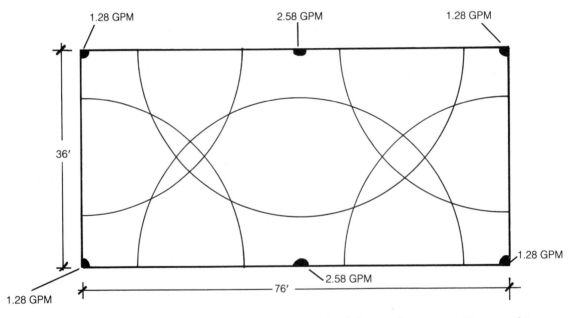

Fig. 2-50. This landscaped area shows six heads. Four are rated by their manufacturer at 1.28 gpm and two are rated at 2.58 gpm.

gpm. The size of the area in square feet is 2628 (73' × 36'). Therefore, you would calculate the inches per hour as follows:

Step 1—Inches per Hour

$$I/H = 96.3 \times \frac{(4 \text{ heads} \times 1.28 \text{ qpm}) + (2 \text{ heads} \times 2.58 \text{ qpm})}{73 \text{ feet} \times 36 \text{ feet}}$$

$$= \frac{(4 \text{ heads} \times 1.28 \text{ qpm}) + (2 \text{ heads} \times 2.58 \text{ qpm})}{73 \text{ feet} \times 36 \text{ feet}}$$

$$= \frac{96.3 \times 5.12 + 5.16}{2628}$$

$$= .3766 \text{ or } .377 \text{ I/H}$$

The 96.3 figure is a constant unit developed by the irrigation industry as follows:

1 gallon of water = 231 cubic inches
1 square foot = 144 square inches

$$\frac{231 \text{ ci}}{144 \text{ si}} = 1.604 \text{ ci/sq.ft.}$$

1.604 ci/sq.ft. × 60 minutes

= 96.3 ci/sq.ft./hr.

Table 2-2. Water Demand.

Plant professionals summarize the general water demand for landscapes as follows:

Plant Type	Amount of Moisture (inches/week)
Lawns	1.5 - 2
Groundcovers	1 - 1.5
Shrubs	1 - 1.5
Trees	1 - 2
Flowers	1 - 2
Vegetables	1 - 3

Table 2-3. Per Minute Operation Calculations.

Take the answer you developed in Step I—Inches Per Hour, the .377 inches per hour figure, and divide 60 minutes into it.

$$\frac{.377 \text{ I/H}}{60 \text{ minutes}} = .00628 \text{ in./min.}$$

This figure converts to .00628 inches of water the sample system will deliver for each minute of operation.

Since lawn grass will require from 1.5 to 2.0 inches of water each week, divide this factor by the .00628 inches per minute, as follows:

$$\frac{1.5}{.00628} \qquad \frac{2.0}{.00628}$$
$$= 238.85 \qquad = 318.47$$
$$= 239^* \qquad = 319^*$$

*minutes of operation per week

Pipe Sizing and Routing. A general piping system will run from the service line that feeds into your property to the first set of valves. From these valves the pipes will run to the next set of valves and then to the sprinkler heads. Most manufacturers suggest using one-inch pipe and valves throughout to reduce pressure loss within a circuit.

The first step in designing your piping system is to locate the valves that will operate the individual circuits. You should group them together for convenience, locating one group for the front yard circuits and another for the backyard circuits.

Design the piping from the valves to the individual heads you have located on your triangular grid or in a specific planting area. You should use as many straight lines as possible. Avoid making turns which might result in friction and loss of pressure. Whenever possible, avoid going under sidewalks or driveways. (See Fig. 2-51.)

Sprinkler equipment manufacturers recommend the following pipe materials for most residential projects:

1. From the water meter to your first set of valves, use copper pipe. It is strong and durable at this point of greatest need.
2. From the first set of valves to the second, use PVC pipe. If your area freezes during the winter months, you must drain this pipe material well.
3. From the second set of valves to the sprinkler heads, use polyethylene. This material is easy to work with in the part of the system which might need the most maintenance. If you live in an area where ground freezing does not occur, polyethylene pipe is suitable throughout your system from the first set of valves to the sprinkler heads. (See Fig. 2-52.)

You can design the necessary trenching network along with your piping system. It should be minimal and contain several circuit pipes to

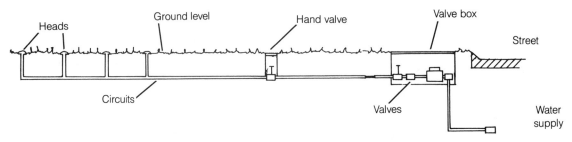

Fig. 2-51. This section represents a typical piping arrangement for a high pressure irrigation system. Illustration courtesy of Buckner Irrigation.

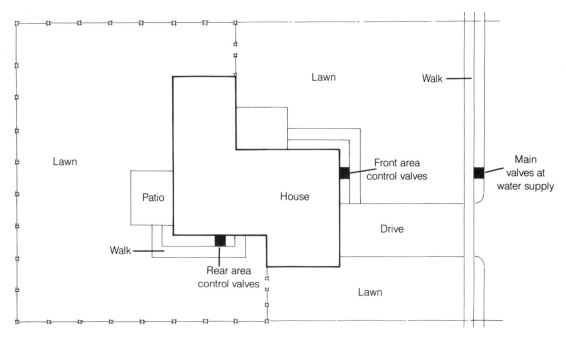

Fig. 2-52. This typical arrangement is for valve boxes, placed out of the way of your lawn activities but in easy reach for installation and maintenance.

avoid unnecessary digging. Use a main trench with smaller lateral trenches to accomplish the least amount of disturbance to your yard. (See helpful hints chart that follows and Figs. 2-53 through 2-58.)

Using these steps and tasks, you now have designed your high-pressure sprinkler system. Your next effort will focus on the selection of the specific products you will purchase for your design. Before you buy your equipment, let's summarize the design of your high-pressure system with an easy-to-follow designer's checklist. This checklist will ensure that you have all the information you need and have considered all the possibilities.

Helpful Hints for Locating Valves.

1. Locate your valve units in groups. One group controlling circuits in the front yard and one controlling the backyard or side areas.
2. Locate your first set of valves in a convenient location near the main water supply. A suggested location is where the main service line enters your house.
3. Use one valve per circuit.

The Designers Checklist.

Step One: Information Gathering

Measuring Water Capacity

a. What is the size of your water meters?_____
b. What is the static water pressure?_____
c. What are the local building codes concerning the installation of underground sprinkler systems?
d. What is the diameter of the service lines leaving your water meter?_____
e. What is your water capacity?_____

Measuring Your Property

a. Does your plot plan show all of the necessary dimensions and features?_____ Compare your drawing to the typical plot plan shown earlier.
   1. All windows have been noted on the plan._____
   2. All adjacent property features have been noted._____
   3. A convenient location for the control box has been noted on the plan._____
   4. True north has been determined._____
b. For existing plant material, you have noted:
   1. The size and height of shrubs._____
   2. Specialty planting areas._____
   3. Tree clumps._____
   4. Tress with low-handing branches._____
   5. Future tree sizes._____

Step Two: Layout and Design

Plot Plan Layout

a. Property is divided into rectangular or square zones for easier head placement._____
b. Each grid shows the spacing pattern._____

Designing Your System

a. Select spray or rotary heads for each zone of your property._____
b. Locate a head for each position on the grid._____
c. Mark the gpm and pressure requirement for each head. _____

d. Locate the valve groupings for the front yard and back-yard._____
e. Draw the piping system from your water meter to the first valve box and to the second valve box._____
f. Draw the individual circuits from each valve to the sprinkler heads._____
g. Draw the trenching system to coordinate the circuit installation._____
h. Itemize the materials you will need for your system. List the heads by type, the valves by size, and the piping by type, size, and length. Use this list to purchase the materials from your local hardware store or building supply dealer.

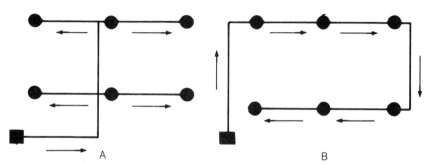

Fig. 2-53. Design your system so that several lines branch from the first head in the circuit (A). Avoid forcing water to travel through too many turns (B).

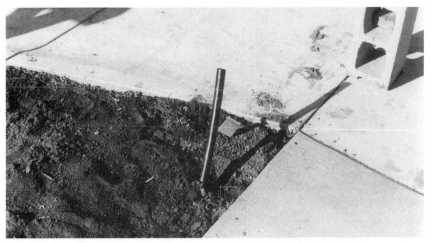

Fig. 2-54. Polypipe often looks like a garden hose entering the ground. If you live in an area that is not subject to hard freezes, you should bury it about six to eight inches deep. For hard freeze areas, a depth of twelve inches is recommended.

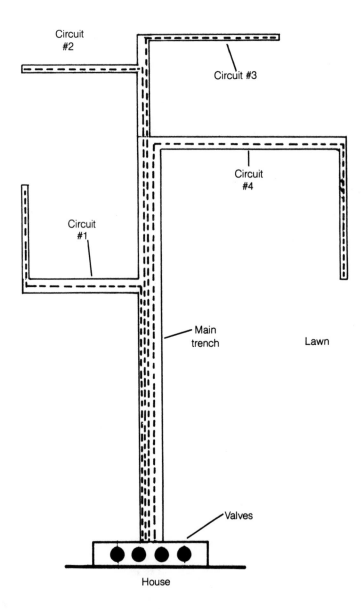

Fig. 2-55. The main trench system should disturb your landscape as little as possible. Use one main trench for as many circuits as possible. Then use a system of smaller trenches for the lateral lines.

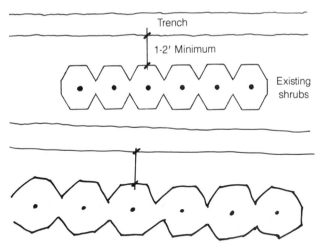

Fig. 2-56. Trench just outside the bed perimeter to avoid damage to delicate root systems.

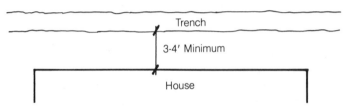

Fig. 2-57. Trench approximately three to four feet away from any permanent structure to avoid damage to the piping network.

Fig. 2-58. Place or pull your polypipe as close as possible to a walk or drive. This will allow you to use a 180 degree arc and not spray water on the concrete.

YOUR MANUAL HIGH-PRESSURE SYSTEM

Basically, you can develop only one type of manual high-pressure system for your lawn. This system is comprised of a quick-coupling valve units connected directly to supply lines. Each of these units is made up of high-impact rotary heads and broadcasts water to a large area of your lawn. It also is possible to connect hoses to these valves and extend the range of a variety of manual accessories.

The Quick-Coupling System—Selection and Placement of Heads. Because of the broad range of coverage by the high impact rotaries, you will need very few heads for this system. A single sprinkler in a strategic spot can provide water to a large section of your property. If your plants are not delicate and you have an ample supply of water, you can accomplish this "water everything" approach easily.

You should locate heads where the radius of throw will cover the largest area of the plants you wish to water. Some waste and overwatering must be expected; however, targeting water to a precise location in your garden is not always possible with this type of system.

Water Supply and Circuiting. The creation of various valve boxes and subsidiary piping networks is not needed. *Quick-coupling units* are valves activated by the insertion of a riser and sprinkler head combination. You easily can attach the supply pipe directly to the main water supply or to an antisiphon valve if local codes require. Electronic controls or other devices are not necessary.

The quick-coupling system is designed once the head units are located and the pipe system is determined. If local codes require, you only need to add the backflow preventer (antisiphon valve). It is a simple system requiring very little technical equipment. The manual requirements are simply the coupling of the head and riser to the underground valve. This activates the system and watering begins. To stop watering, remove the head and riser unit.

Checklist procedures for the quick-coupling system are similar to those presented earlier. Instead of marking the gpm and pressure for each head, however, you simply locate the single head unit. The gpm and pressure will be quite adequate for only one head. Locating valves and valve boxes is not necessary, nor is an elaborate circuit or a trenching system.

Your equipment list for the quick-coupling system will be much shorter than for an automatic system. You might, however, want to add several pieces of hand watering accessories if you feel they are necessary.

The section on sprinkler equipment illustrates the various hand watering devices that are available in most stores. (See Figs. 2-59 through 2-60B.)

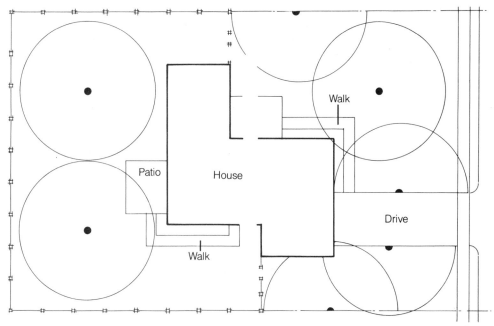

Fig. 2-59. This design illustrates the coverage pattern of a quick coupling system. Fewer head units are required, but the quick coupling system uses more water than other types.

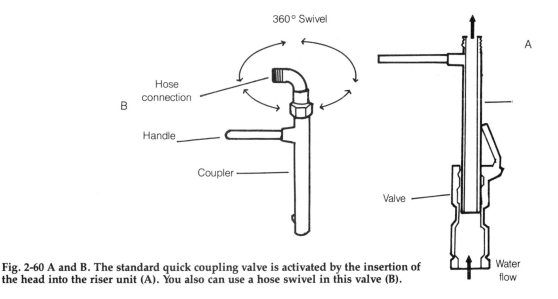

Fig. 2-60 A and B. The standard quick coupling valve is activated by the insertion of the head into the riser unit (A). You also can use a hose swivel in this valve (B).

THE DRIP IRRIGATION SYSTEM

The second type of manual irrigation is the drip system. It is actually a hybrid between the fully automatic high-pressure system and the fully manual garden hose. You can install it above or below ground and it has a wide range of flexibility for both ornamental landscapes and native gardens. It has a specific application to smaller landscapes found in condominiums, and you easily can apply it to apartment patio gardens. (See Figs. 2-61 through 2-70.)

In order to design a manual system for your lawn, follow the initial steps used for the automatic system. Gather the base information and measure your property carefully. Convert this information to a working plot plan and divide your property into watering areas, as before.

This concept for lawn irrigation has been in operation for centuries. Long before electricity, hydraulics, and plumbing equipment, farmers and gardeners used gravity to move water slowly throughout their plantings. When pressured piping came along, drip watering remained popular for watering display gardens and unique ornamental landscapes. As technology advanced, many gardeners felt that broadcast watering was faster and more effective. This concept remains true only if water is plentiful and is not rationed or under the restrictive control of government agencies.

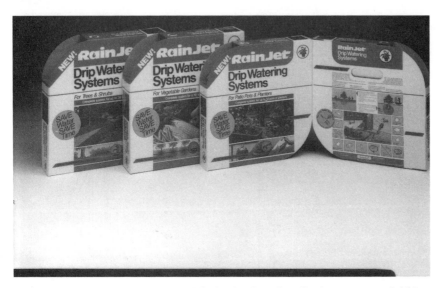

Fig. 2-61. Drip irrigation systems might be developed easily from commercial kits. Everything needed to water trees, shrubs, vegetable gardens, and patio gardens is provided. Photo courtesy of James Hardie Irrigation.

Fig. 2-62. The Turbo-Key Emitter drip head applies water at a slow rate to the plants in your garden. Photo courtesy of James Hardie Irrigation.

Fig. 2-63. You can place the emitter head at the end of a micro-tube hose and mount it on a stake.

Fig. 2-64. The E-2 emitter head fits under delicate plants to apply water directly to the base. Photo courtesy of James Hardie Irrigation.

Today's lawns and landscapes, however, are under more stress and strain from external sources. Neighborhoods are growing; municipal watering capabilities are limited; and pressures on homeowners to use less water is expanding. The newly developed manual drip systems might be the forecast of the future.

The specific benefits of the drip irrigation system are as follows:

- Less water is needed to maintain plant growth. Because you apply the water slowly and continuously, the actual amount of water that reaches the plants is applied more efficiently.
- Less energy is needed to operate the system. Because of its low pressure requirement, electrical energy is not needed to trigger valves or control boxes.
- Plant growth is improved. Underground drip systems are able to deliver moisture directly to the root systems of plants. This method creates a more even and attractive habit of growth.
- This system is adaptable to most small garden environments. You no longer are required to have large lawn areas with shrub masses and tree groupings. It is applicable to conventional home landscapes, native plant gardens, and apartment patio plantings.

Fig. 2-65 A and B. Micro sprinkler heads operate under low pressure and deliver water in a full or partial circular pattern. You can attach it to a standard riser unit (A) or mount it on a fixed shrub spike (B).

Fig. 2-66 A, B and C. Installing a drip hose a few inches underground is very easy. Use a shovel to dig a small trench next to the hose (A). Place the hose at the bottom of the trench (B). Cover it over with soil and you will not see it in your garden (C).

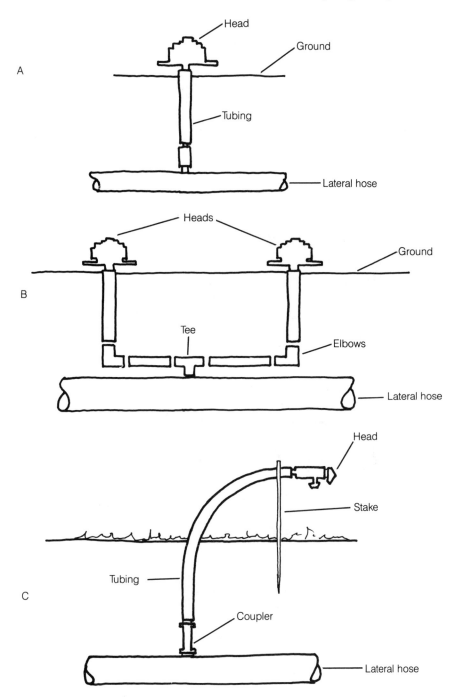

Fig. 2-67 A, B and C. You can attach heads from the lateral hose in several ways. A = Single Outlet; B = Double Outlet; or C = Directed emitter. Illustrations courtesy of James Hardie Irrigation.

A

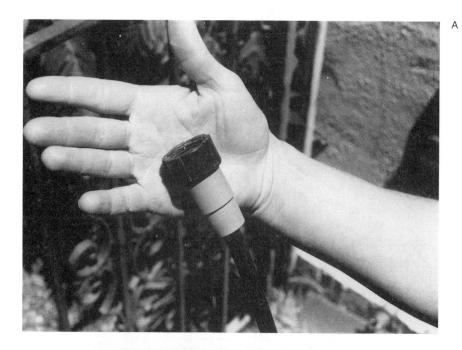

B

Fig. 2-68 A and B. Some drip systems have manual hose attachments for ease of operations.

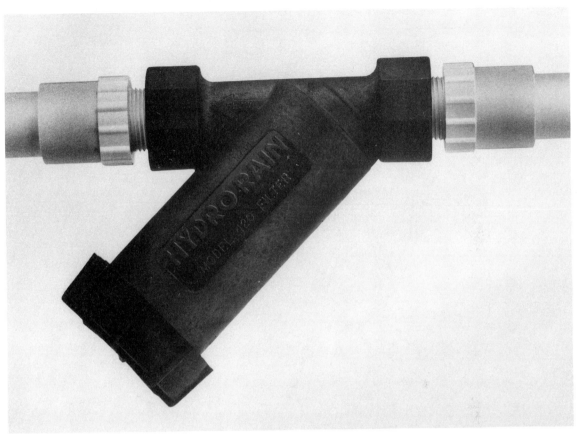

Fig. 2-69. An inline system filter is easy to install and is recommended as standard equipment for your drip system. Photo courtesy of James Hardie Irrigation.

Selection and Placement of Drip Heads

You should select the heads for the drip system based upon the types of plants you have in your landscape. Commercial kits are available for lawns containing trees and shrubs. Separate kits are available for vegetable gardens and even kits for patio pots and container plantings. The various heads available will interchange among the systems, based primarily on your specific need (see Table 2-4.)

Four basic heads are available for drip systems. First, the *mister* or *fogger* delivers a fine spray or mist at close range to delicate and sensitive plants. Ferns and wildflowers will no longer be weighted down from too much water if you use this head. You can apply moisture directly to the surface of the plant with minimal damage to its structure.

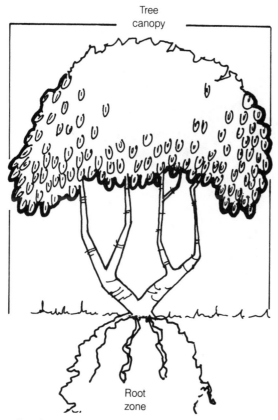

Tree
canopy

Root
zone

Fig. 2-70. The main advantage to the drip system is that it supplies moisture to the root zone of the plant material. Route heads and hoses carefully near the base of the plant.

Table 2-4. Drip Head Comparison.

I—Mister Heads

Circuit Length	Number Heads	
	1/4″ Hose	1/2″ Hose
10′ - 25′	3	8
26′ - 50′	5	30
51′ - 75′	5	50

II—Low Volume Heads

Circuit Length	Number of Heads
10′ - 50 ′	20
51′ - 75 ′	30
76′ - 100′	35
101′ - 125′	30

(Information courtesy of Rainbird Sales, Inc.)

You would use misters more for commercial nurseries than residential landscape systems. Their ability to deliver fine droplets of water under higher pressure make them very effective when plants need wet leaf surfaces. If you decide to use a mister head on a patio area, they should be on a separate circuit. Any decrease in pressure created from other types of heads on the same circuit might reduce the ability of the nozzle to mist properly.

Second, the *emitter head* provides moisture to the plant's soil base in a slow and steady drip. You can use single emitter heads in combination with foggers for container gardens. Plants might never require hand watering. Usually you place these heads close to the ground which helps deliver moisture directly to the root system.

Third, the *micro-sprinkler head* throws water in a small radius under low pressure. You would use these heads predominately in ground-cover beds and mass shrub plantings where conventional heads cannot apply proper moisture. When you place them on mounted or movable stakes, they are adjustable to fit the needs of the garden more easily than stationary heads.

The emitter head and the micro-sprinkler head are low-volume units and are best for small lawn areas or ground-cover plantings. Use each type on its individual circuit.

Fourth, the *micro jet head* will throw a circle of water up to ten feet in diameter. Because of its low pressure requirements, the stream of water is less likely to vaporize before reaching the lawn. You can expect some loss with any head, but this unit is designed to function with minimal loss.

Head Location. When determining the location of each of the drip heads, place them next to your plants. If you have more plants on one side of your lawn, use more heads in that area. With fewer plants, use fewer heads. Because the system is so precise, head location becomes a matter of choice and not an equipment requirement. As your garden grows and changes, your head location can change without a complete redesign.

Water Supply and Circuiting. One of the most convenient aspects of the drip system is the lack of technical apparatus. The kit connects directly to an existing hydrant, and you can move it if necessary to the front, side, or back lawn areas. An antisiphon valve connects to the hose unit and you can control the pressure by a small, preset pressure regulator. Circuiting is not required because the heads are operating under such low working pressure.

Hose Sizing and Routing. For most low-pressure, manual drip systems, the hose requirements are very simple. You need to only consider two sizes, each readily available at hardware or building supply stores. The main supply line is about one-half inch in size. It connects to the hydrant and extends to the locations where water is to be delivered. From this hose you add microtube hoses, about one-eight to one-quarter in size. These hoses run laterally from the main supply hose to the individual head components. You can remove and reconnect the microtubes as required to make your drip system quite flexible.

Follow the same checklist for drip systems as you do for the automatic system. Simply modify it as needed for the different system parts.

3

Installing Your System

FOR THE DO-IT-YOURSELFER, YOU CAN COMPLETE THE INSTALLATION OF A home lawn sprinkler in six easy steps. Based upon your completed plot plan and design, each step will progress until the system meets your needs. You can accommodate changes or redesigns with these procedures. Nothing is final until you, the sprinkler owner, decide that it is finished. The six steps in this process are:

1. Locating and pinning the valves, heads, and trenches.
2. Locating and installing the sprinkler supply valves.
3. Locating and installing the main circuit control valves and automatic timer.
4. Trenching and installing the sprinkler circuits.
5. Installing sprinkler heads.
6. Testing the system.

Locating and Pinning the Valves, Heads, and Trenches

Pinning your system will indicate visually the location of each of your selected components. By visually connecting each pin, you will be able to see how the trenches will connect to each sprinkler head. (See Figs. 3-1 through 3-2B.)

First, pin the location where your property's water supply connects to the city water main. Mark this stake "main supply" on the side and push it firmly into the ground. At this location, you will install an important set of valves and special piping units. (See Fig. 3-3.)

Fig. 3-1. Before you begin your construction, it is best to make a visual check of your design to make sure everything you want will be in its desired location. Purchase a package of pins from a building supply or hardware store. These pins are light and movable and will indicate the location of each element.

Next, stake the location for the main controlling valves. If you have a large property, you might need to use remote control valves for each circuit. If your property is small, you might wish to place your control valves in a group at this location. (See Fig. 3-4.)

Now that you have located the controlling centers for your system, you can locate each of the sprinkler heads as indicated on your design. Place a pin at each head position. Write on the side of the pin the type of each sprinkler head. Mark all the heads similarly in your design.

Once you have located each important valve and head on your property, recheck your design to make sure you are watering all of your landscape. Take a string the length of a typical radius of throw for a sprinkler head and walk the circle to see where the water will spray. If you feel a change is necessary, you can make it easily at this step.

If no changes are required, it is time to mark the location for the piping trenches. Using your string, connect the main supply pin to the MCV pin. This string marks the main supply trench for your system. From the *MCV* (Main control valve) pin, place a string to each of the sprinkler heads on a single circuit. If you need a remote control valve for

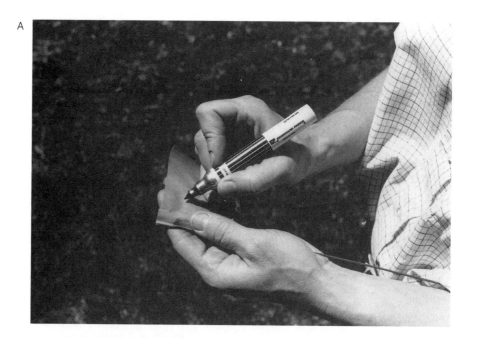

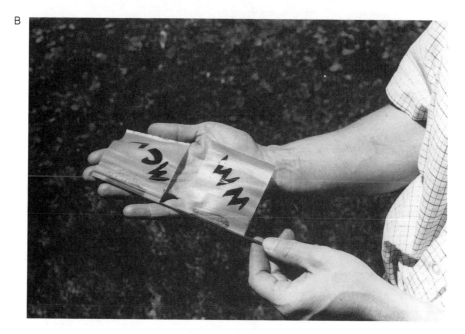

Fig. 3-2 A and B. You might wish to mark the flags on the pins with head, valve, or meter codes so you will be able to see each location.

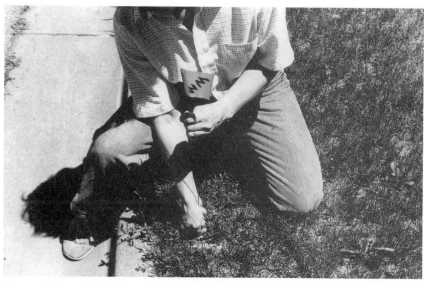

Fig. 3-3. Place a flag pin next in the street curb where the city water connects to your supply valve. It might be enclosed in a box or located just below the surface.

Fig. 3-4. Place a pin where you will locate your main system control valves. Your initial supply pipe (and trench) will run in a straight line from the city water supply to this point on your property. Avoid placing it where obstructions might interfere with this straight trench.

a distant circuit, run a string from the MCV pin to it and mark the pin RCV. At this step, you can locate common trenches to save digging and piping materials. (If you are installing an automatic system, you also should mark a trench from the main circuit valves to the system timer box. This box usually is located in a garage or other protected structure.) (See Figs. 3-5 and 3-6.)

Fig. 3-5 A and B. Before you begin to dig the trenching system, place a pin where each sprinkler head will be. This pin will provide you with a visual check of your design before you begin construction (A). The open lawn head should help you check the radius of throw of the heads (B). The pins next to new groundcover plantings will help adjust the radius.

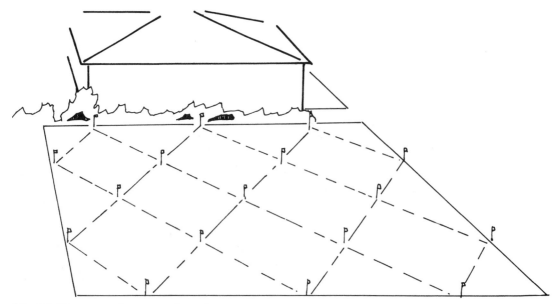

Fig. 3-6. Pin your entire system throughout your landscape. Check this final layout with your design. Make any changes at this point to avoid costly errors later.

Locating and Installing the Sprinkler Supply Valves

At the pin labeled "main supply", you will need to install a compression tee, a shutoff valve, a drain valve, and a back-flow preventer. Some cities might require you to make a special correction at this location. Others might require that a licensed plumber install these devices. Check your local codes before you begin this initial installation; however, once you have them installed, it will be easy to install the rest of the system. Follow these directions to do it yourself:

- Use the valve near the water meter to cut off the water supply.
- Cut into the supply line where convenient.
- Remove a section of pipe, leaving space large enough to accommodate a compression tee.
- Slip the tee over each end of the cut pipe.
- Tighten the compression nuts. The rubber gasket will compress against the pipe, creating a seal to prevent leakage.
- Install a short section of pipe coming out of the tee.
- Attach a shutoff valve and then a back-flow preventer to this section of pipe. The shutoff valve allows you to turn off the system manually if necessary.

Information courtesy of The TORO Company.

Following are the installation instructions for a compression tee and shutoff valve in the basement:

- Turn off your water supply.
- Cut into the service line after the water meter and insert a compression tee.
- Drill a hole through the wall above the foundation. Make the hole no bigger than needed to run a 1-inch pipe through it.
- Install the piping as shown. Add a shutoff valve and drain plug. The drain cap should be in a low position to allow for winterizing.
- Run your connecting pipe out of the basement to the outside to where the back-flow preventer and the first set of valves are located.
- To drain water from the system, close the shutoff valve, place a bucket under the drain cap, and remove the cap.
- Be sure to seal the hole in the wall with caulking compound after installing the connecting pipe.

Information courtesy of The TORO Company.

Follow these easy directions for a typical installation using an outside faucet as the main water supply system:

- Remove the faucet.
- Install a 1-inch galvanized or copper tee.
- Reattach the faucet with a close nipple.
- Attach a male adapter to the tee; install the shutoff valve; and run the pipe from the valve to the sprinkler system.

Information courtesy of The TORO Company.

You can arrange these various components according to the way the main water supply enters your property. You might install them below ground next to the water main or arrange this network in your basement or, you might connect them next to an outside faucet. Any method will be acceptable, however, in most hard-freezing areas, the first two methods are recommended. (See Figs. 3-7 through 3-10.)

Locating and Installing the Main Circuit Control Valves and Automatic Timer

Following the pin line from the main supply to the MCV pin, dig a trench approximately 12 inches deep. It can be less than 12 inches in areas where ground freezing is not a problem. If you must dig under a

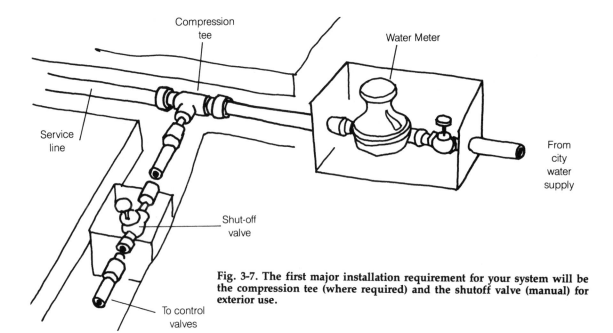

Compression tee

Water Meter

Service line

Shut-off valve

From city water supply

To control valves

Fig. 3-7. The first major installation requirement for your system will be the compression tee (where required) and the shutoff valve (manual) for exterior use.

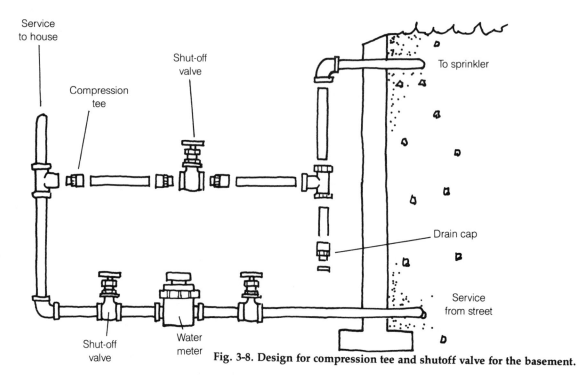

Service to house

Shut-off valve

Compression tee

To sprinkler

Drain cap

Service from street

Shut-off valve

Water meter

Fig. 3-8. Design for compression tee and shutoff valve for the basement.

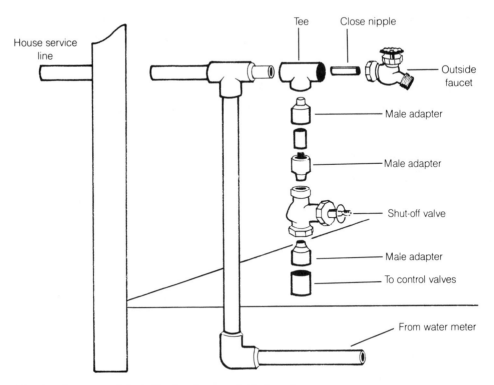

Fig. 3-9. System and shutoff valve for an outside faucet.

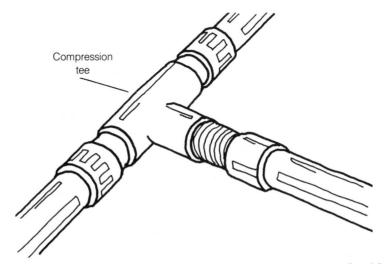

Fig. 3-10. A compression tee will allow you to connect to your water supply without soldering. Illustration courtesy of The TORO Company.

driveway or walkway, use a hose and pipe assembly to drill under the concrete or just tap a ridged pipe through the ground in a tunneling effect. (See Fig. 3-11.)

Attach your main sprinkler supply line from the sprinkler supply valves to the first set of control valves. Some city codes might require this pipe to be copper. If copper is not required, PVC might be substituted. You should use boxes to protect the first set of valves. You might buy a ready-made plastic valve box or build one from high-quality redwood. Either material is adequate.

For your automatic system, you will need to locate and install a timing device. Follow these steps to include this component in your piping network.

- Locate the timer in your garage or some other convenient place. An adequate power supply is necessary for the controller to operate properly. Each manufacturer has stated this requirement for their respective controller.
- Run wires along a trench from the timer to the main circuit valves.
- Use the instruction sheet that comes with your timer to connect the valves to the controller.

Fig. 3-11. In the early stages of your construction, locate your timer in a convenient, protected area. This garage location is excellent for most systems.

- Test the system by electronically opening and closing each valve in sequence. The manufacturer's instructions outline the single steps for this procedure.
- Refill the trench and replace the sod.

Trenching and Installing the Sprinkler Circuits

From the main circuit control valve, dig a trench along the string to each of the heads. Be sure the trenches are deep enough to accommodate the sprinkler. If adjustments are required in the circuits, you can make them at this time. Lay the pipe alongside the trench and place a reducer tee or elbow at the appropriate location next to the sprinkler head. (See Figs. 3-12 through 3-18.)

Install the connecting PVC or polypipe network to conform to your sprinkler system design. Cut the pipe with a hacksaw to the desired length. Clean the pipe surface at each joint location. For PVC material, brush pipe solvent (cement) on the outside of the pipe end and to the inside of the fitting unit (reducer tee or elbow). Slip the pipe into the fitting and give it a quarter turn. Hole it in place about 20 seconds so the solvent can dry. Wipe off the excess solvent with a rag. You will need to wait approximately one hour before running water through the system. This timing will allow the solvent to set and permanently bond the joints together. (See Fig. 3-19.)

If you are using polypipe, attach it to your PVC supply line using a standard adapter. After this attachment, you will no longer need the special solvent to connect the joints. You can clamp polypipe together with a

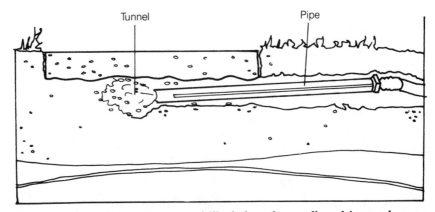

Tunnel   Pipe

Fig. 3-12A. If you discover you must drill a hole under a walk or driveway, here are two methods that will help. Use a garden hose attached to a long piece of pipe. The force of the water will act as a drill to provide a trench for your pipe. Illustration courtesy of The TORO Company.

Fig. 3-12B. For shorter distances, use a large hammer and 1-inch pipe. Information courtesy of James Hardie Irrigation.

Fig. 3-12C. Force a 1-inch pipe underneath the walk.

Fig. 3-13. If you decide to dig your trenches by hand, remove the grass and soil and place it carefully on top of plastic liners. This procedure will allow you to recover all of the materials you have removed. Continue to dig along the string line until you reach the head location. Information courtesy of James Hardie Irrigation.

Fig. 3-14A. If you decide to use a trenching machine for those areas of your system with polyethylene pipe, make sure there is adequate room for maneuvering. The small tractor-mounted machine is available from many equipment rental outlets.

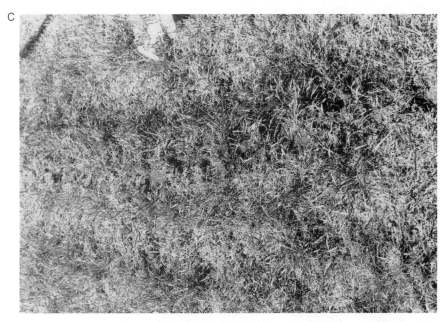

Fig. 3-14 (B) The attachment on the machine makes a small slit in the ground which allows the flexible pipe to be pulled along the circuit system. (C) The slit is hardly visible after cutting.

Fig. 3-15. The back-flow preventer is one of the most important units of your irrigation system. It is a heavy brass unit designed and built to last for many years. It prevents contaminated water in your system from reaching the city water supply. A licensed plumber might be required to install this unit. Check your city codes on the regulations for this important element.

Fig. 3-16. Most city codes require a copper pipe between the city main and the back-flow preventer.

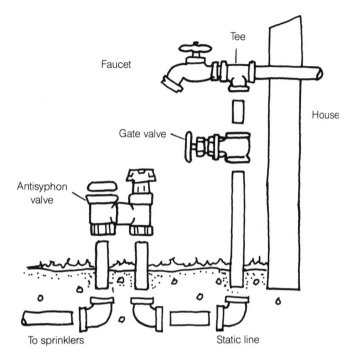

Fig. 3-17. **Some systems will allow you to connect the back-flow (also called an antisyphon valve) directly to an outside faucet. If you have a small landscape project and adequate pressure (usually above 40-50 psi), this method might be best for your design. This configuration works best if you have a least a ³/₄" service line to your faucet. Illustration courtesy of James Hardie Irrigation.**

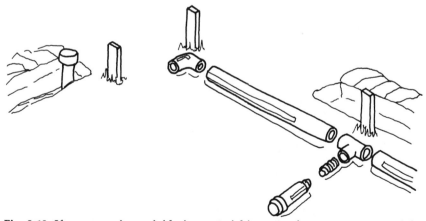

Fig. 3-18. **If you are using a rigid pipe material in parts of your system, you might wish to lay each component out on top of the ground first. This will give you a visual picture of the system. Recheck your design with this layout and make corrections where necessary. Illustration courtesy of The TORO Company.**

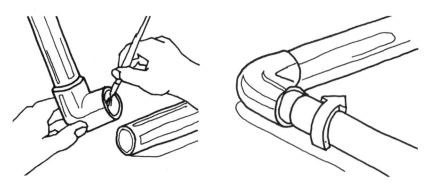

Fig. 3-19. Some locations within your system might require the use of PVC piping materials. If so, you must use a bonding agent to secure the joints. Simply apply the solvent to the inside of the joints, insert the pipe, and twist a quarter turn. Hold it in place until dry (about one minute). Wipe off excess solvent. Illustration courtesy of The TORO Company.

standard pipe clamp and tighten it with a screwdriver. Make sure your clamps are tight as detailed by your manufacturer's specifications. (See Fig. 3-20.)

At a low point in each circuit, attach an automatic drain valve. This simple device will attach to a reducer tee and empty through a short section of pipe into a bed of packed gravel. When your sprinkler system shuts off, the automatic drain valves open and release water so that no water is standing in the pipes at any time. This procedure is very important, especially in areas where freezing is a problem. (See Figs. 3-21 and 3-22.)

Installing the Sprinkler Heads

Once you have installed the connecting pipe network, it is time to install the sprinkler heads. At each reducer tee or elbow, place the appropriate riser. Attach each riser to a tee or elbow. If the riser is too high, cut a portion off using a knife. Once you have attached these risers firmly, it is time to test and flush the system. Flushing is an important step in cleaning the network of any debris accumulated during installation. The flush procedure should be as follows:

- Seal each interim riser with pipe plugs. Leave the riser unplugged at the end of the circuit.
- Turn the water on, open the main control valves, and flush the system until the water runs clean.
- Remove the pipe plugs and let the water run from each riser.

(See Figs. 3-23 through 3-26.)

A

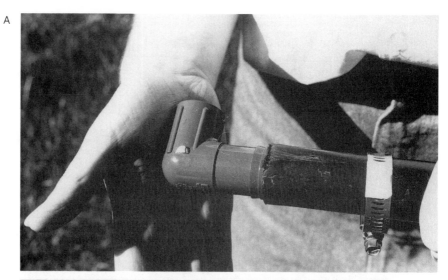

B

Fig. 3-20 A and B. When required, connect the poly material to the PVC material as follows:

- Cut the polypipe with a clamp cutter or hacksaw.
- Clip a stainless steel clamp over the end of the polypipe (A).
- Insert the fitting into the end of the pipe.
- Slide the clamp over the ridges of the fitting.
- Tighten the clamp.

NOTE: Do not use polypipe as the connecting pipe between the service line and control valves. Surge pressure might rupture polypipe.

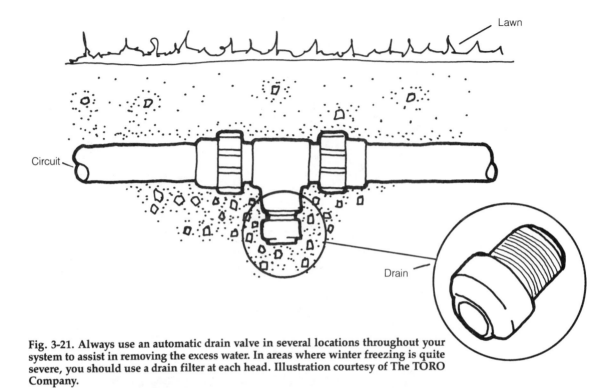

Fig. 3-21. Always use an automatic drain valve in several locations throughout your system to assist in removing the excess water. In areas where winter freezing is quite severe, you should use a drain filter at each head. Illustration courtesy of The TORO Company.

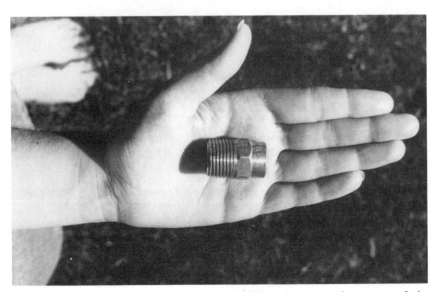

Fig. 3-22. The automatic drain valve is very small but plays a very important role in protecting your system.

Fig. 3-23. The head riser component is an adjustable plastic riser and is the link between the pipe network and the head units.

Fig. 3-24. Riser/Pipe Connection—The hard, plastic riser connects to the hard, plastic pipe joint to assure maximum strength from the pressure within the system.

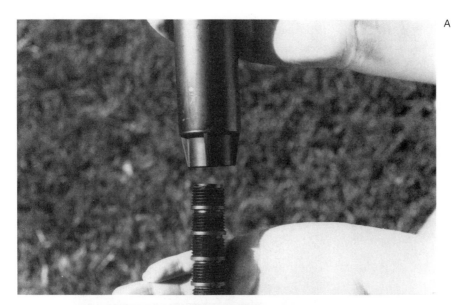

A

B

Fig. 3-25 A and B. Riser/Head Connection—The threads of the riser component connect to the threads of the head (A). The riser allows the pipe to be buried below the frost line (B).

Attach the appropriate sprinkler head to the riser. Make sure your pop-up heads (if used) are set flush with the ground. If necessary, cut the riser to adjust the head height.

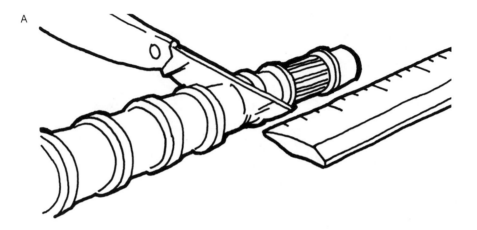

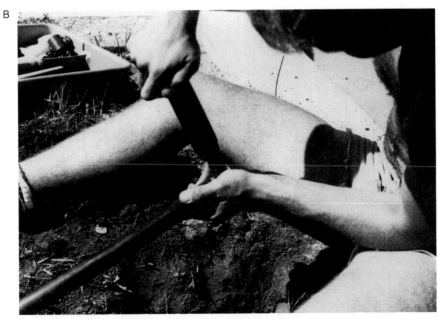

Fig. 3-26A and B. The plastic riser can be cut with a knife to the desired height (A). Illustration courtesy of The TORO Company. The head can be measured easily for proper height (B).

C

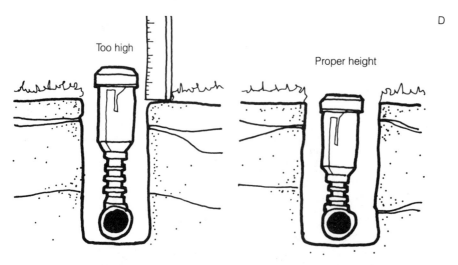

D

Too high

Proper height

Fig. 3-26C and D. When completed (C), the components become a working part of an active system. Pay careful attention to the height of the head in relation to the surface of the ground (D).

Testing the System

Before you backfill the trenches, tie each sprinkler head to a stake placed at the bottom of the trench. Check the operation of your system as follows:

- Turn off any water being used in the house.
- Turn on the waste to your system and open the control valve. Do this for each circuit—one at a time.
- Adjust the screws on the sprinkler heads to fine tune the spray patterns.
- If coverage is not complete, go back to your system design. You might need to select different heads to provide more adequate coverage.
- Once satisfactory coverage is reached, backfill the trench and replace the sod.
- Repeat each step for every circuit.

Quick Coupling System

You install the quick-coupling system in a similar fashion to the automatic system, only it has fewer control valves. You only need to follow these steps to complete this type of manual system.

- Connect to the main supply in the same way you would an automatic system. You will need to have a shutoff valve, compression tee, and back-flow preventer. For this system, too, your city might require a licensed professional for installation.
- Instead of a control valve, you will trench and pipe directly to the quick-coupling valve. It also will require a riser for the proper height, and an automatic drain valve to remove the standing water. However, since there are no control valves, your automatic drain valve will function only when your system is closed by the shutoff valve.
- Test your system by inserting a quick-coupling head into the valve to activate the system. Use only the head riser to first flush the system. Replace the head when the water is clear.
- If you have achieved the coverage desired, backfill the trench and replace the sod.
- Repeat the steps for each quick-coupling valve and head.

Drip System Installation

The manual drip system takes even fewer steps than the quick-coupling system. Because of the convenient kits that are available, most of the components are ready to install. Depending upon your requirements, you can place the tubing network on top of the ground, or install it just below the ground, about three to four inches. Follow these easy steps to complete your manual drip system: (See Figs. 3-27 through 3-31.)

- Locate the water source nearest the area to be watered. If you have more than one area, you can install a second kit without a great loss of pressure.
- Unroll the kit hose and place it beside the areas to be watered. Do not bury the hose at this time. The decision to place it above or below the ground will be made in a later step. This one-half inch hose becomes the main supply line for your manual drip system. Lateral lines or tubing will be connected to this component to deliver water to the plant materials.
- Place sections of the smaller tubing at the positions where heads

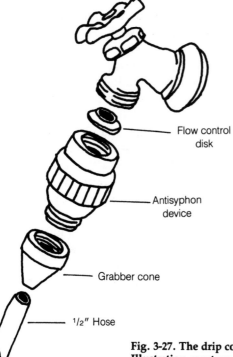

Flow control disk

Antisyphon device

Grabber cone

1/2" Hose

Fig. 3-27. The drip components connect directly to the hydrant. Illustration courtesy of James Hardie Irrigation.

will be located. Cut these sections with a pair of scissors or a knife. All cuts should be square.

- Using the materials provided in the kit, connect the unit to the water source. Most of these materials will include a flow control disc, an antisiphon unit, and a connector. Make sure they are adequately sealed to prevent leakage. Leaving the end of the hose open, flush the system by running water through it for about 3 to 5 minutes.

- Along the main kit hose, punch a hole in the side at each location where you will install tubing. Use the hole punch apparatus provided with the kit.

- Attach the drip strip connectors to the main kit hose, and insert the tubing to these connections. You can use these hose sections to deliver water to the more remote areas of your landscape. By punching holes in its base, you can use this strip hose as a drip system. Water will then drip into the garden a small amount at a time.

- If you prefer to connect the various heads directly to the main kit hose, punch a hole in the hose at the location where you will place a head. Place an adapter in the main kit hose hole. Attach a length of one-quarter inch tubing to the adapter and run this tubing to the head location. Leaving the ends of the tubing open, run water through the system for about 1 to 2 minutes.

- Select the type of head you want from the various items in the kit. Depending upon the type of watering method you desire, you might choose a drip emitter, a micro jet sprayer, a micro sprinkler, or a mister/fogger. Test your system. Make adjustments in the head locations as desired.

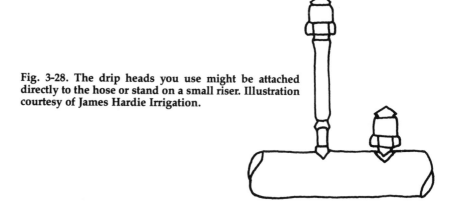

Fig. 3-28. The drip heads you use might be attached directly to the hose or stand on a small riser. Illustration courtesy of James Hardie Irrigation.

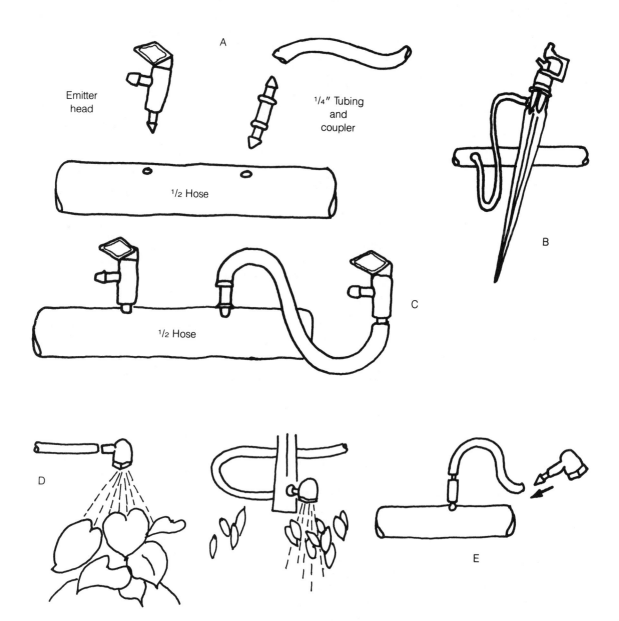

Emitter
head

¼" Tubing
and
coupler

½ Hose

½ Hose

A

B

C

D

E

Fig. 3-29. Drip Head Varieties. Courtesy of James Hardie Irrigation.

A) **Emitter heads are flexible on hoses or micro tubing.**
B) **Micro-jet head on a movable stake.**
C) **Mister/Fogger head on micro tube.**
D) **Mister/Fogger head for upward spray.**
E) **Mister/Fogger as foliage sprayer.**

Now you have installed a fully operational irrigation system for your landscape. These materials represent the state of the art in lawn irrigation.

The following helpful hints will help you operate your drip system more efficiently:

- Your drip system requires clean, filtered water because of the small outlet on the various heads. If you use well or spring water, you must adapt a filter unit to your system.
- If you use your system above ground, hold the hose in place with hose stakes. If you place your hose underground, do not bury it more than 6 inches. Do not place the one-quarter inch tubing beneath the ground.
- If you use emitter heads at the base of small and medium shrubs or trees, they should be located halfway between the trunk and the drip line of the plant.
- You should flush the drip systems once each month during the operational period. Each flushing will require the removal of the heads. In areas of hard ground freezing, remove and store the kit properly.

Appendix A
Water Supply
Comparison Chart

WITH THE INFORMATION YOU HAVE GATHERED ON THE SIZE OF YOUR WATER meter, the diameter of your service line, the length of your service line, and the psi for your property, use one of the charts in Figs. A-1 through A-3 to determine how much water is available for your landscape. (Charts courtesy of James Hardie Irrigation).

Based on 50' Supply

Water meter	Supply line	Control valve	System pipe	30	35	40	45	50	55	60	65	70	75
5/8"	3/4"	3/4"	3/4"	3/4"	4.5	6.6	8.1	9.4	10.5				
5/8"	3/4"	3/4"	R.J.	4.7	6.8	8.4	9.8	11.0					
3/4"	3/4"	3/4"	3/4"	4.8	6.9	8.5	9.9	11.1	12.2	13.3	14.3		
3/4"	3/4"	3/4"	R.J.	5.0	7.2	8.9	10.3	11.6	12.8	13.9	14.9		
3/4"	3/4"	3/4"	1"	5.6	8.0	10.0	11.6	13.0	14.5	15.5	16.6		
3/4"	1"	3/4"	3/4"	5.6	8.1	10.0	11.6	13.0	14.3	15.5	16.6	17.7	18.7
3/4"	1"	3/4"	R.J.	6.0	8.6	10.6	12.3	13.8	15.2	16.5	17.6	18.8	19.8
3/4"	1"	3/4"	1"	7.1	10.1	12.5	14.5	16.3	17.9	19.3			
1"	1"	3/4"	3/4"	5.6	8.1	10.0	11.6	13.0	14.3	15.5	16.6	17.7	18.7
1"	1"	3/4"	R.J.	6.2	8.9	11.0	12.8	14.4	15.8	17.2	18.4	19.6	
1"	1"	3/4"	1"	7.6	10.9	13.3	15.5	17.3	19.0	19.4			
1"	1"	1"	R.J.	6.9	10.0	12.4	14.4	16.2	17.9				
1"	1"	1"	1"	8.7	12.5	15.5	18.0	20.1					
1"	1 1/4"	1"	R.J.	7.4	10.7	13.2	15.4	17.3	19.0	20.6			
1"	1 1/4"	1"	1"	9.7	13.9	17.1	19.9						

Fig. A-1. Chart to determine availability of water for your landscape (Courtesy of James Hardie Irrigation).

Based on 100' Supply

Water meter	Supply line	Control valve	System pipe	30	35	40	45	50	55	60	65	70	75	80	85
5/8"	3/4"	3/4"	3/4"		3.9	5.6	7.0	8.1	9.1	10.0					
5/8"	3/4"	3/4"	R.J.	4.0	5.8	7.2	8.4	10.4	11.2						
3/4"	3/4"	3/4"	3/4"	4.0	5.8	7.2	8.4	9.5	10.4	11.3	12.2	12.9	13.7		
3/4"	3/4"	3/4"	R.J.	4.2	6.0	7.5	8.7	9.8	10.8	11.7	12.6	13.4	14.2		
3/4"	3/4"	3/4"	1"	4.6	6.5	8.1	9.4	10.6	11.7	12.7	13.6	14.5	15.3		
3/4"	1"	3/4"	3/4"	5.3	7.6	9.4	10.9	12.3	13.5	14.7	15.7	16.7	17.7	18.6	19.5 1"
3/4"	1"	3/4"	R.J.	5.6	8.0	9.9	11.5	13.0	14.3	15.5	16.6	17.6	18.6	19.6 3/4"	
3/4"	1"	6.5	9.3	11.5	13.3	15.0	16.5	17.8	19.1						
1"	1"	3/4"	3/4"	5.5	7.9	9.8	11.4	12.8	14.1	15.2	16.4	17.4	18.4	19.3	
1"	1"	3/4"	R.J.	5.8	8.3	10.3	12.0	13.5	14.8	16.1	17.2	18.3	19.4		
1"	1"	3/4"	1"	6.8	9.8	12.0	14.0	15.7	17.3	18.7	20.1				
1"	1"	1"	R.J.	6.4	9.2	11.4	13.2	14.9	16.4	17.8	19.1				
1"	1"	1"	1"	7.6	11.0	13.7	15.9	17.9	19.7	20.0					
1"	1 1/4"	1"	R.J.	7.1	10.3	12.8	14.9	16.7	18.4						
1"	1 1/4"	1"	1"	9.2	13.2	16.2	18.9								

Fig. A-2. Chart to determine availability of water for your landscape (Courtesy of James Hardie Irrigation).

Based on 150' Supply

Water meter	Supply line	Control valve	System pipe	30	35	40	45	50	55	60	65	70	75	80	85	90
5/8"	3/4"	3/4"	3/4"			5.0	6.2	7.2	8.1	9.0	9.7	10.4				
5/8"	3/4"	3/4"	R.J.	3.6	5.2	6.4	7.4	8.3	9.2	10.0	10.7	11.4	12.1			
3/4"	3/4"	3/4"	3/4"	3.5	5.1	6.4	7.4	8.4	9.2	10.0	10.7	11.8	12.4			
3/4"	3/4"	3/4"	R.J.	3.6	5.3	6.6	7.7	8.6	9.5	10.3	11.1	12.5	13.2			
3/4"	3/4"	3/4"	1"	4.0	5.6	7.0	8.1	9.2	10.1	10.9	11.7					
3/4"	1"	3/4"	3/4"	5.0	7.2	8.9	10.4	11.7	12.8	13.9	15.0	16.0	16.8			
3/4"	1"	3/4"	R.J.	5.2	7.5	9.4	10.9	12.3	13.5	14.6	15.7	16.7	17.6			
3/4"	1"	3/4"	1"	6.0	8.7	10.7	12.4	13.9	15.3	16.6	17.8	18.9	20.0			
1"	1"	3/4"	3/4"	5.1	7.4	9.2	10.7	12.0	13.2	14.4	15.4	16.4	17.4	18.3	19.1	19.9
1"	1"	3/4"	R.J.	5.4	7.8	9.6	11.2	12.6	13.9	15.1	16.2	17.2	18.2			
1"	1"	3/4"	1"	6.3	9.0	11.1	12.9	14.5	16.0	17.3	18.6	19.8	20.0	19.1	20.0	
1"	1"	1"	R.J.	5.9	8.5	10.6	12.3	13.9	15.3	16.6	17.8	18.9				
1"	1"	1"	1"	6.9	10.0	12.4	14.4	16.2	17.9	19.4	20.8					
1"	1 1/4"	1"	R.J.	6.9	10.0	12.4	14.4	16.2	17.8	18.4						
1"	1 1/4"	1"	1"	8.7	12.5	15.6	18.0	20.1								

Fig. A-3. Chart to determine availability of water for your landscape (Courtesy of James Hardie Irrigation).

Appendix B
Maintenance Program

A MAJOR CONSIDERATION OF YOUR IRRIGATION MAINTENANCE PROGRAM IS preparing the system for winter. In areas of severe ground freezing, this will protect the valuable components and extend their operation capacity. Proper winterizing begins with an understanding of how your system works and how it has been designed.

Well located drains will help remove the standing water from your system. This removal is very important in areas where the ground freezes beyond 6-8 inches in depth. Freezing water within a system will cause the components to crack, requiring replacement.

Other ongoing maintenance should include the following:

- Flushing.
- Coverage Adjustments.
- Valve Maintenance.
- Operation Clearing.

Flushing

You should remove individual nozzles and heads periodically to allow the system to be flushed. Flushing removes the dirt and debris that might collect in the risers or pipe system. After removing these elements, turn the water on for a few minutes until a clean, solid stream flows from the heads. Turn the water off and replace the nozzles and heads. (See Fig. B-1.)

A

Fig. B-1A and B. To clear clogged spray heads, you might occasionally need to remove the nozzle. Dirt and debris often prevents them from working properly (A). A clogged pop-up sprayer will remain in the upright position when clogged (B).

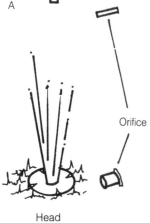

Orifice

Head

B

Coverage Adjustments

From time to time, the coverage patterns will be disturbed. This disturbance will include the overlap between heads and the quarter and half circle patterns. To correct these patterns, remove the head and readjust the radius of throw. Some units have adjustment screws that you can turn to correct the pattern. (See Fig. B-2.)

Valve Maintenance

If water is noticed leaking from one of the valves in your system, this usually indicates debris is inside the component. A rapid opening and closing of the unit might dislodge the debris. If not, you might have to remove the cap and blow out the unit with compressed air.

Operation Clearing

Grass and ground covers are a constant problem for pop-up and stationary spray units. You must clip these materials every few weeks to maintain good operation. Stream rotors, on the other hand, have enough force to push tall growing grass aside. Clipping also will be required for these heads, but less often. (See Figs. B-3 and B-4.)

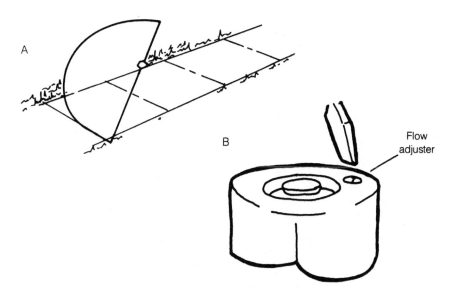

Fig. B-2 A and B. Heads often get bumped or kicked and knocked out of alignment. When this happens, water might be sprayed onto a walk or drive creating a hazard (A). Some heads have adjustment screws that allow easy direction changes (B).

Fig. B-3 A and B. The most common problem with spray heads is grass. Clip this growth regularly for efficient performance (A). Rotary heads usually will keep the grass pushed down (B).

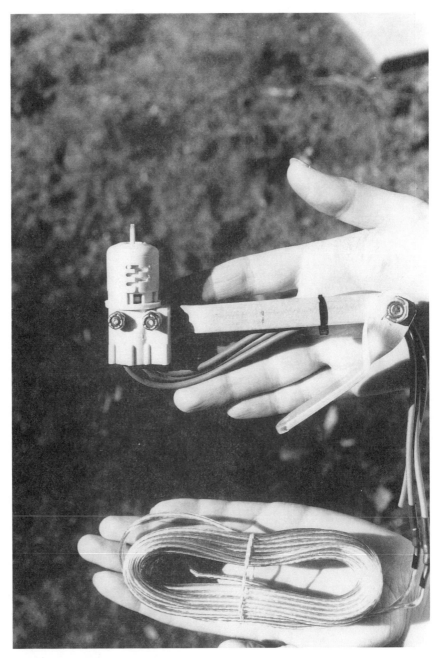

Fig. B-4. For a fully automatic system, a rain sensor will help maintain proper operation. This unit senses when the system is not needed due to excessive rain and shuts the system off.

Appendix C

MANUFACTURERS/EQUIPMENT SUPPLIERS

JAMES HARDIE IRRIGATION
27671 La Paz Road
Laguna Niguel, CA 92656
714/643-0444
800/423-2379

BUCKNER IRRIGATION SYSTEMS
4381 N. Brawley Ave.
Fresno, CA 93722
209/275-0500

THE TORO COMPANY
Irrigation Division
5825 Jasmine St.
Riverside, CA 92504
714/688-9221

RAIN BIRD SALES, INC.
Turf Division
145 N. Grand Ave.
Glendora, CA 91740
818/963-9311

Glossary

Angle Valve a valve which causes water to flow at a 90-degree angle from which it enters.

Anti-Siphon Device a device to prevent contamination of drinking water by water in sprinkler system lines.

Application Rate the amount of water applied to a given area of landscape in one hour, measured in inches per hour.

Arc of Coverage the degrees of coverage of a sprinkler head from one side of the throw pattern to the other. A 90-degree arc of coverage would be a quarter circle. A 180 degree of coverage would be a half circle.

As-built Plan a complete plan of an installed lawn irrigation system designating the exact location of all system components. Includes all of the changes made in the original plan during the installation process.

Automatic Control Valve a sprinkler system valve activated by an automatic controller.

Automatic System a lawn sprinkler operated by an electric control box, preset by the homeowner.

Backflow the unwanted reserve flow of liquids in a lawn sprinkler piping system.

Backflow Preventer a mechanical device within a lawn sprinkler system that will allow water to flow in one direction but will not allow water to flow in a reverse direction.

Battery of Sprinklers a specific group of lawn sprinklers controlled by one valve.

Brackish Water water which is contaminated or polluted by organic matter, salts, or acids.

Check Valve a valve which permits water to flow in one direction only.

Controller the automatic timing device for a lawn sprinkler system and its enclosure.

Coverage the general term applied to the manner in which water is applied to the landscape area.

Cycle refers to a complete operation of the controller timing device.

Design the drawn recommendation for the use of sprinkler system components.

Distribution the manner in which a lawn sprinkler system applies water to the landscaped area.

Distribution Pattern the pattern of water application of a specific type of sprinkler head over an area of lawn.

Drain Valve a valve used to drain water from an irrigation line to remove pressure from the system or to prevent freezing in winter.

Electric Valve an automatic lawn sprinkler valve usually controlled by 24 to 30 volts of AC current.

Emitter a device used in drip irrigation to deliver water to an area of the landscape under low pressure.

Evaporation the loss of water from the lawn sprinkler system into the atmosphere in the form of a vapor.

Flow the movement of fluids through pipes and valves in a lawn sprinkler system.

Flow Switch a device which controls the output of a pump within a lawn sprinkler system.

GPM abbreviation for gallons per minute.

Groundwater water found below the surface of the ground.

Head-to-Head Spacing the placement of lawn sprinkler heads in such a manner that the radius of throw from one sprinkler strikes the adjacent sprinkler.

Hose Connection Vacuum Breaker a device used to protect against back-siphonage in a low pressure manual system.

Main a large pipe sized to carry water to a home. Lawn sprinkler systems are not usually connected to the main.

Manual System a lawn sprinkler system in which valves are opened manually rather than by automatic control valves.

Mist Irrigation the application of water to a landscape, garden, or greenhouse area in the form of very small drops (or mist).

Operating Cycle   refers to a complete run of a controller through all of its programmed stations.

Operating Pressure   the pressure at which a lawn sprinkler system will operate most effectively.

Overlap   the coverage into an area of a landscape by more than one sprinklers.

Precipitation Rate   the rate at which lawn sprinklers apply water to a landscape.

PSI   abbreviation for pounds per square inch.

PVC Pipe   a semiridged plastic pipe in general use in lawn irrigation systems.

Polyethylene Pipe   a black, flexible pipe common used in home lawn sprinkler systems.

Potable Water   water that is intended for human consumption.

Pressure   the force per unit area measured in pounds per square inch (psi).

Pressure Loss   the loss of pressure energy under water flow conditions caused by pipe friction or directional changes within the irrigation system.

Program   the watering plan or schedule for your sprinkler system.

Quick-Coupling System   a type of manual lawn irrigation system with underground valves and hand-activated sprinkler heads.

Quick Coupling Valve   the valve used in a manual quick-coupling system.

Rate of Application   the rate at which water is applied to your landscape area by the sprinklers within a specific pattern.

Riser   a length of pipe affixed to a system pipe line for the purpose of supporting a sprinkler head or valve.

Sleeve   a pipe through which another pipe or wiring is run, usually under a walk or driveway.

Spacing   the specific distance between sprinkler heads.

Sprinkler   a hydraulic device that distributes water through a nozzle or orifice.

Static Pressure   the pressure (psi) within a closed lawn sprinkler system.

Underspace   the term used to describe the situation where sprinkler heads are spaced closer than they need to be for effective operation.

Valve-In-Head   a term used to describe a sprinkler head assembly which has an automatic control valve as part of the sprinkler assembly.

Valve-Under-Head   a term used to describe a lawn sprinkler system which has an automatic control valve under each head assembly.

Velocity   a speed at which water travels through a lawn sprinkler system.

Index